The barrier to entry for online ministry i[...]
From Social Media to Social Ministry, [...]
use social technology for much more than we have in the past. With
her perspective as a global thought leader in this space, she shows us
that online ministry is more than an opportunity. It's a responsibility.

Bobby Gruenewald, founder of YouVersion

Nona has been pioneering in social media ministry for years. *From Social Media to Social Ministry* is not only incredibly rich and deeply practical but also extremely timely. There has never been a better time to shift our thinking from social media to social ministry, and Nona leads the way.

Carey Nieuwhof, bestselling author, podcaster, and speaker

Nona Jones occupies a uniquely critical role in the ecosystem of the twenty-first-century church. *From Social Media to Social Ministry* is prophetic and prescriptive and a must-read for those who are serious about cultivating a relevant and effective ministry.

Jamal Harrison Bryant, senior pastor of
New Birth Missionary Baptist Church

Nona is a visionary. In a time of massive digital disruption within the church, she brings together her lifelong experience in ministry and her knowledge of social technology to help the church strengthen community and bring people deeper in their faith. *From Social Media to Social Ministry* uncovers the power of using social technology for discipleship. It is a must-read.

Troy Pollock, chief ambassador at Pushpay

Nona Jones's knowledge, experience, and insight into social media and its ability to impact the world of ministry is unparalleled. Her work has influenced and helped engage our ministry in ways beyond what I ever imagined.

John K. Jenkins Sr., senior pastor at First Baptist of Church of
Glenarden, chair of the National Association of Evangelicals

You can't spend much time with Nona Jones without the Great Commission being mentioned. Her passion for the church's mission and expertise in how we can use social technology to fulfill it has made her an authority, both as a minister of the gospel and as a pioneer in the technology sector. She has proven to be accessible and strategic in the way she has partnered with local churches to further the gospel.

Doug Clay, general superintendent of the
General Council of the Assemblies of God

Nona Jones has a voice the kingdom of God needs to hear; she guides us to the next level of social media. This book provides an extraordinary wealth of practical information that is certain to become one of the most utilized reference guides on the subject. Keep this one close!

Robert E. Coleman Jr., director of public
relations at Church of God in Christ, Inc.

Social media has revolutionized the way we all do ministry today, creating opportunities both locally and globally to accomplish our goals and objectives. Nona has continued to be the leading voice in this space, introducing the concept of social ministry and bringing practical application of social media that has led to exponential ministry impact. I'm so grateful for her stepping into this moment and cannot wait for you to read this profoundly insightful book.

Nils Smith, chief strategist social
media+innovation at Dunham+Company

Nona's prophetic insight into social ministry could not be more timely. In the age of digital (and church) revolution, *From Social Media to Social Ministry* is a must-read for every Christian and leader who is passionate to see God's kingdom increase.

David L'Herroux, CEO of United Christian
Broadcasters (UK) and European regional director

Nona has the unique ability to couple her passion to reach people with a social strategy that is necessary for the fulfillment of the Great Commission. I would highly recommend you read this book and share it with your team to gain fresh insight into expanding your influence in the digital age.

Shaun Nepstad, pastor of Fellowship Church, ARC Churches Board of Directors, and author of *Don't Quit in the Dip*

Nona Jones is a front-runner in digital discipleship for the church. She has been instrumental in pushing the global church forward. If you're a church leader or want to know how to shift your own understanding of discipleship, pay attention to what Nona is teaching.

Katie Allred, founder of ChurchCommunications.com, assistant professor at University of Mobile

Nona Jones has written the primer for pastors and church leaders who want to evolve their work in a digital-first world. This book is for anyone thinking through how to use social media successfully in their ministry. Read this book—and learn from one of the best.

Kenny Jahng, CEO of Big Click Syndicate, founder of ChurchBuilder.com

Nona Jones has long been championing the need for ministries—regardless of size—to awaken to the reality that the church is more than a building: it's the people. And the people have gone online. *From Social Media to Social Ministry* explains not only why digital ministry matters but also how to do it.

Tayo Ademuyiwa, cofounder of Givelify

FROM SOCIAL MEDIA TO SOCIAL MINISTRY

FROM SOCIAL MEDIA TO SOCIAL MINISTRY

A GUIDE TO DIGITAL DISCIPLESHIP

NONA JONES

ZONDERVAN
REFLECTIVE

ZONDERVAN REFLECTIVE

From Social Media to Social Ministry
Copyright © 2020 by Nona Jones

Requests for information should be addressed to:
Zondervan, *3900 Sparks Dr. SE, Grand Rapids, Michigan 49546*

Zondervan titles may be purchased in bulk for educational, business, fundraising, or sales promotional use. For information, please email SpecialMarkets@ Zondervan.com.

ISBN 978-0-310-10386-8 (softcover)
ISBN 978-0-310-10402-5 (audio)
ISBN 978-0-310-10401-8 (ebook)

Cover design: Rick Szuecs Design
Cover image: © liravega258 / 123RF
Interior design: Denise Froehlich

Printed in the United States of America

21 22 23 24 /LSC/ 10 9 8

*To everyone who has a vision for
kingdom impact that is bigger
than four walls can contain*

Contents

Introduction

The Moment Everything Changed

When I first began working at the intersection of faith and social technology in August 2017, I was surprised to learn that churches were significantly underrepresented when it came to using social technology for discipleship. Pastors and church communicators uniformly viewed it as nothing more than a tool to get people into their church buildings. I saw massive potential to help people come into faith and deepen their faith through social technology, so early on I made it my mission to shift the paradigm about what church is. The rate of people attending worship services was declining year after year while the proportion of people identifying as a religious "none" was increasing.

My efforts were often met with interest, but actual change rarely followed. In fact, on February 3, 2020, Barna Group released its 2020 State of the Church report that revealed trends in how pastors were thinking, and when asked what was on their minds, the very last thing was "trends in online church and digital technology." Then, shortly after the report was released, media outlets around the world began to report that a new deadly virus was decimating people's health in Wuhan, China. Most people didn't pay much attention to it early on, but then a case was discovered outside China, and health officials became concerned.

I was scheduled to head to London in the middle of February, and when I finished packing my bags, my husband turned to me and said, "Be careful. I hear that coronavirus is starting to spread." While I was in London, there was a palpable sense of growing concern because cases were being discovered in Italy. I left London with a sense that something was about to break. After I returned to the US, I had several meetings in the Bay Area, then I was scheduled to speak at an event in Seattle. But as I was wrapping up my meetings in the Bay Area, I received an alert from the organizers in Seattle assuring me that the coronavirus situation was being taken seriously. I hadn't been watching the news, so I did a quick internet search for "coronavirus and Seattle" and found that several deaths had happened in the area and it was now considered a virus hot spot. At the same time, I received a warning from my travel team telling me to return home as it was becoming unsafe to travel.

Once I made it home and began to take stock of the situation, I learned there were more and more reports of people testing positive for the virus around the country. Government leaders were beginning to get worried and started to consider measures to quarantine people and communities. The NBA cancelled their season after a player tested positive for the virus, and cases began to mount, causing local authorities to place restrictions on in-person gatherings. Conferences and events were being cancelled one by one like dominoes falling, and suddenly, pastors who had anchored their ministry approach to people coming to a building for service were confronted with the unexpected need to figure out how to gather without a building.

I received panicked emails, texts, messages, and phone calls from people all around the world who needed immediate guidance on how to move their services online. The most obvious solution was livestreaming on Facebook and YouTube, but as preventative measures became more stringent and people were told to stay home from work, school, and all activities indefinitely, the issue was no longer just about streaming the service. It became about how to do church entirely online. I started writing this book in summer of 2018, well before the outbreak, and the principles it contains will *outlive* the outbreak. In this age, church online is no longer an option; it's an imperative. But what I hope people now understand is what I have believed all along; church is more than the worship service. It is the community of people gathered together under the banner of Jesus Christ's lordship, and fully leveraging social media for discipleship requires making the leap from social media to social ministry. Let's get started.

PART 1

The
Why

CHAPTER 1

Numbers Don't Lie

I started writing this book before it had a title. I knew what I wanted to write about, but there wasn't a concise way to describe the book. I had spent the year and a half prior to writing it immersing myself in the possibilities of leveraging Facebook for ministry. I had watched as some churches and organizations applied my strategies to their ministry models and succeeded, and I also watched as other churches and organizations scoffed at my strategies in favor of "quick hit" campaigns that ultimately fizzled over time. I started receiving invitations to speak at more church communication conferences than I could possibly attend, so I determined that the best way to scale myself and share my message with the masses would be to put it in a book. But what to call it? One day I was walking out of my home office to run an errand when I heard "from social *media* to social *ministry*" in my spirit. It so clearly and rightly described what I was trying to convey that I stopped in my tracks and said, "exactly," out loud—to no one.

Finally, I could describe in two words what I had been working on and what was in my heart: *social ministry*—helping churches go beyond using social technology to build their brand to using social technology to build God's kingdom. I knew it was going to be a radical concept for some because social media is largely viewed as an advertising platform: a quick, cheap, and often free way to broaden reach and to get butts into seats on the weekends. Never mind that the first word in the phrase is *social*; many church leaders and communications professionals were initially hesitant to imagine social technology as anything more than a mechanism to broadcast information.

At this point I've consulted with countless denominations, local churches, and Christ-centered charities, and the one thing they all had in common at the start was a desire to grow their reach. "How do we get more followers?" "How do we get more people to like our posts?" "How do we get more people to support us financially?" In other words, "How do we better leverage social media to market ourselves?" When I examine the life of Jesus, however, I notice something different. He didn't make the twelve apostles stand at crossroads and ask people to come listen to him preach in the temple on the weekends. He didn't turn his followers into a "street marketing team" that would hang scrolls around town telling about his next sermon series. He didn't deploy flocks of doves to airdrop invitations to his next baptism. Instead, he was out among the people, making *connections* and having *conversations*. All day, every day.

There are 168 hours in a week, but most local churches focus 90 percent of their resources on one to two hours on

He was out among the people, making *connections* and having *conversations*.

Sunday morning, leaving people to figure out the other 166 to 167 hours on their own. Even in the face of COVID-19, the first question on most pastors' minds was, "How do we stream our service?" Yet the life of Jesus flies in the face of this model. He didn't reserve his best blessings, healings, prayers, and teachings for the temple. He met people where they were and ended up unleashing a global movement after only three years of public ministry. This is why I believe if Jesus were on social media today—besides having the supercool, Instagram-and-Facebook-verified handle @JC—I believe he would be calling the Church to move beyond simply sharing content to making disciples. He would be calling us to move from social media to social ministry. And this requires a radical paradigm shift in how we do ministry today.

We must become less concerned about the number of likes we get on a post and the number of views we get on a video and more concerned about the number of lives that were changed *because of* them. I wrote this book with the goal of getting you to the latter while equipping you to do the former—with purpose. If the only reason you want more followers or views is because it makes you feel better about yourself, you've missed the entire point. It doesn't matter how many followers you have if those followers aren't following Jesus. So I invite you to join me as we together catalyze a ministry movement that no longer sees social technology as a threat to church attendance but understands it as a strategic lever for kingdom advancement. My ultimate prayer is that everything shared in this book will equip you to make disciples of all nations—right from your fingertips.

The Numbers

There are more than 350,000 churches registered in the United States today, and two out of every three are declining or plateauing in attendance.[1] Pastors noticed this trend years ago but assumed (hoped) it was simply an anomaly that could be fixed with a few structural tweaks. Churches that weren't growing added earlier and later service times

It doesn't matter how many followers you have if those followers aren't following Jesus.

to better fit with what were believed to be the crammed schedules of members and prospective visitors. Many churches even began hosting "satellite" church services at various locations around town, thinking people would come to a service if it was closer to their home. But as new times and locations were added, something unexpected happened. Instead of new people attending, the people who had been faithfully attending simply went to services at different times or locations. The solution didn't solve the *problem* because the solution didn't fit the *cause*.

The 2018 General Social Survey (GSS) produced by Eastern Illinois University found that more people now identify as "no religious affiliation" (23.1 percent) than evangelical Christian (22.6 percent) or Catholic (23 percent).[2] This shift is happening while more and more megachurches—churches with average weekly attendance of two thousand or more—appear to be popping up every month. Studies have even shown that as more churches around the country are becoming the "fastest-growing churches in America," more and more cities are becoming less and less "churched."[3] We have more megachurches and fewer professing Christians. We have more service options and fewer in overall attendance. But the reason adding service times and locations has not solved the problem of church attendance is because it is a symptom of a much larger problem: *we live in a post-Christian society.*

Post-Christian is defined as the loss of the preeminence, or primacy, of the Christian worldview in places where Christianity previously flourished. This is especially true in Western culture, the United States in particular, a

As more churches around the country are becoming the "fastest-growing churches in America," more and more cities are becoming less and less **"churched."**

place believed to be founded by Christians on Christian principles. In lieu of a Christian worldview, post-Christian societies tend to favor alternative worldviews such as secularism, nationalism, environmentalism, and more. Indicators of a post-Christian society include dramatically decreased percentages of people who pray, study the Bible, claim a religious affiliation, and *attend church*. When the GSS disaggregated the data on religious affiliation (or lack thereof) to understand how generational differences accounted for the way people identified themselves, they found that the generation leading the pack of "no religious affiliation" is the generation churches seem most concerned with reaching: millennials. And they are followed closely by their children, gen Z. The Pew Research Center's surveys showed that over the last ten years, the percentage of Americans who identify as Christian has dropped twelve percentage points.[4] And lest you missed that, allow me to clarify. It didn't drop 12 percent. It dropped 12 percentage *points*, from 77 percent of the US population to 65 percent. *This is major.*

Why the rapid decline? Why are people leaving Christianity or not showing up at church on the weekends? Well, according to many of the millennials surveyed by the Pew Research Center and GSS who chose "no religious affiliation," the answer lies in one word—*relevance*. Or to put it more plainly, *lack* of relevance. Merriam-Webster's dictionary defines *relevance* as "relation to the matter at hand," as well as "practical and especially social applicability." So when millennials say Christianity specifically, and religion generally, isn't relevant to their lives, they are saying it doesn't relate to their priorities and isn't integrated into their everyday lives.

In response to this reality, many churches have essentially "dressed down" their church services. They've added coffee shops, removed crucifixes, built LED video walls, put on ripped jeans, and put away Bibles. While those cosmetic tweaks did lure some new people in, the bait hasn't kept the new fish in the bowl according to the Pew Research Center. Yet again, the solution hasn't solved the problem because the solution didn't fit the cause.

Have you ever had somebody say, "I would attend your church, but do you have free coffee?" Or how about, "I would attend your church, but I need light shows and smoke machines to really feel the Spirit." Have you ever invited someone to church only to have them say, "I don't do church. The last time I was there, I was shocked and offended to find a Bible on my seat." I'm going to take a wild leap into the dark and guess that the answer for all three scenarios is no. The data doesn't link a decline in attendance to any of those things. The data links the decline to one main thing: a perceived lack of relevance. And relevance isn't only a question of your message; it's also a question of your method.

Deconstructing a "Successful" Church

"I've been struggling to grow beyond one hundred members for the past five years, and I feel like a failure. I see all of these large churches in my city and wonder what I'm missing."

The pastor was genuinely exasperated as he looked me in the eyes. My heart ached as I listened to him. I had just finished speaking at a conference in Charlotte, North Carolina, and stayed around to greet people. He was no more than forty and told me he came to the conference to try to learn some new strategies to grow his church because nothing he had been doing up to that point had worked. "I'm ready to quit. I wonder all the time if I called myself to pastor instead of God calling me, because it just seems like God's favor isn't on my church. I need help. Hope, really." After five years of pastoring, he felt his one hundred–member church was an anomaly, but what he didn't know was that he was actually in the majority.

Although multisite, multicity, multiday, multitime megachurches are the ones getting all the publicity, research shows that almost 60 percent of local churches have fewer than one hundred people in attendance each weekend, with only 11 percent having greater than 250.[5] The research also shows that the smaller churches are dying while the larger churches are growing. But the growth isn't happening through new conversions. Seventy-seven percent of the people who join growing churches are already Christians, and many had a previous church home that they left. In other words, the vast majority of local church growth is driven by local church death.

The vast majority of local church **growth** is driven by local church **death.**

The pastor who felt like a failure because he compared his church's lack of growth with the growing churches around him needed a new definition of success. The growing churches around him were filling up with the people leaving his church and other churches, not the increasing number of people who aren't connected with a church community. According to Gallup, 40 percent of Americans report attending church on any given Sunday, but actual attendance is closer to 20 percent.[6] Given this, I would like to offer a few important thoughts for your consideration.

The church has become an aquarium. There are two kinds of church: the "big C" Church and the "little c" local church. The "big C" Church is what Jesus referred to in Matthew 16:18 when he shared that he would build his church upon the rock. He wasn't referring to a local church building; he was referring to the global, monolithic body of believers who would follow his teachings and surrender their lives to his plan. House churches (little c) became the local organizing mechanism by which the "big C" Church gathered, but it was never God's plan for the growth of the local church to supersede the growth of the "big C" Church. This is why when Jesus called his first two disciples in Matthew 4:19, he said, "Come, follow me . . . and I will send you *out* to fish for people" (emphasis mine).

To fish for people requires going *out* into the deep. It requires *leaving behind* what's familiar in favor of what's promised. But many have become so comfortable inside four walls that when church attendance drops, instead of going out to fish, many churches just try to keep the other fish in their aquariums from leaving too. In most cases, church growth is not a result of going out to catch new fish; it's merely fish jumping from one aquarium to another.

The church has left the building. As a local church pastor myself, it never ceases to amaze me that people I may not have seen in church or heard from in years will see me out grocery shopping and thank me for being their pastor. When I tell them how much I miss seeing them, they inevitably say, "Oh, I'll be back soon. Just a lot going on in my life right now. But I watch you every week on Facebook, and you've blessed my life."

How is it possible that a person who hasn't darkened the door of our church in months or years could still view me as their leader? Simple. Technology. You used to have to attend a worship service to participate in the worship and hear the message, but now livestreaming has allowed people to stay connected with a local church despite being unable to physically attend (or choosing not to because they have more important things to do, such as . . . sleep in).

If 40 percent of Americans say they attend church services every weekend but only 20 percent are showing up, that means 50 percent of the people who say they attend your church aren't actually showing up to weekend worship services (and every pastor on earth nods in agreement). Raising the question of "to livestream or not to livestream" is the fastest way to watch a group of kindhearted pastors degenerate into a discussion as fierce as a presidential debate, but spoiler alert: you *must* livestream—but as part of a comprehensive social ministry strategy. More on this later.

Church is no longer a place. Google Insights reports that every month, more than thirty thousand people search

Google using the phrase "church online." This means people are actively searching the internet to connect with a community of faith that doesn't require getting into a car to drive to an address. Part of the reason so many brick-and-mortar retail stores have had to file for bankruptcy is because online sales have replaced an astronomical percentage of in-store purchases. Many retailers were unprepared for the transition, so they simply continued business as usual until business was too unusual to continue. One of the first retailers to fall was Blockbuster. Then Circuit City, with Sears and Toys "R" Us only limping along after bankruptcy, and on and on. These companies staked their future on the idea that the internet was a passing phase and that people would want to walk into a building and interact with their products before purchasing. They were wrong.

The internet is not just a "thing" people do; it's the place people live, especially millennials and gen Z. Generations that have known only a life with the internet and social media. Generations that don't often realize you can call people on a smart phone. Generations that will sit around a dinner table during a night out with friends, while each person is on their own phone, not speaking to anyone else. Being alone . . . together. If the church experience continues to be limited to a physical address you visit, when today's generation lives online, the trends will only get worse.

A Paradigm Shift

I care deeply about the Church. My personal story is one of faith and redemption because of a local church. So please hear me when I say the Church and local churches must adapt, or we will die. Some have framed technology and church as an "either/or" proposition where you have either in-person church or online church, but I don't see it that way. I see it as "both/and." Let's look again at the life of Jesus for a moment. Jesus taught both in the temple and on the street corners. Jesus prayed both in the temple and with people in need whom he found along his journey. Jesus didn't limit his ministry to a location or a method, and we can learn a lot from the one who started it all.

When I first started in my role at Facebook, I remember speaking with the social media director of one of the five largest churches in America. After I shared my vision of equipping churches to use the platform for digital discipleship, she said, "Oh, we're not interested in that. We use Facebook to get people into the building. That's our main goal for social media." Although that was disappointing to hear, it was also very illuminating.

For her and many others, the purpose of social media is to drive people to the building, to get "butts in seats." For many people, church is what happens on a date, at a time, at a physical address. It's the program that takes place between 11:00 a.m. and 12:15 p.m. It's scripted and has rehearsals and teams and plans that are timed to the second. But herein lies the philosophical difference between a social media *plan* and a social ministry *strategy*. A social media plan focuses on getting people to the building for a couple of hours every weekend, whereas a social ministry strategy focuses on how to help them grow in their faith through social technology after they leave. You need both, and if you focus only on a social media plan, you will build an audience while stopping short of building disciples.

An audience is passive. It's a group of people gathered together to watch or listen to something. I'll be the first to admit that having a few thousand people watching you and listening to you speak is exhilarating and humbling. And after I finish, I always feel a lingering question: Did they get it? Every communicator worth their salt wants to equip listeners to live their best lives, but when we speak to them for only thirty minutes once a week, how can we be sure they understood what we tried to convey? How can we be sure that the time we used to prepare was well spent? In working with churches around the world, I've discovered a common thread in their loudest message on social media: "Come to our church on Sunday!" The one message that rises above all others is the request that people come to the building. But what if they don't show up? And *the data already shows that they're not showing up.* Has our definition of ministry become so focused on the building that we can't change lives outside of it?

Church Isn't Church Unless I See You There

With every technological innovation, church leaders have braced themselves for a mass exodus because technology makes access to information easier. When the printing press was created and copies of sermons became more widely available, preachers assumed people would skip church or revivals in favor of reading the message later. When radio was invented, preachers were afraid to air sermons out of fear people would stop showing up and would instead listen later. When television became mainstream, pastors were reluctant to join the bandwagon because giving people the ability to watch from home would surely decrease church attendance. When the internet picked up steam, many churches refused to have a website, preferring that people call and get information from a live person. When social media became a way of life, pastors refused to create an account, citing, "I don't want everyone in my business." When livestreaming took off, many pastors denounced it as another option to keep people at home and away from church.

At every juncture of technological advancement, naysayers have resisted the change only to fall in line with it after it was too late and a new development was on the rise. I've talked with my share of people who have a lot of angst around the idea of "online church," not only because it's a novel idea but because they don't believe it's possible to build an authentic church community online. While I believe COVID-19 forced everyone off a cliff they may not have been wearing a parachute for, I want to offer two thoughts because there are still quite a few leaders who have said, "I can't wait to go back to normal church." First, I've been a member of and leader in small churches, and one thing I know for sure is that you can be in a small church and still feel invisible. Whether you build an authentic church community is less a question of the modality of church and more a question of the intention of the church. Some members of megachurches feel deeply connected to their church while being one of tens of thousands, while some members of small churches are on the brink of leaving because they don't feel connected to their church while

You can be in a small church and still feel **invisible**

being one of tens. Given this, church community—Christian community—is a culture we create regardless of where it happens: big church, little church, online, or in person.

Second, the fear that online church will replace in-person church is simply not rooted in data. Research doesn't show that people aren't attending church because they're watching at home. It shows that people aren't attending church because they don't feel it's relevant to their lives. Furthermore, the people who feel that way aren't watching your livestream, so streaming your service won't keep new people away or make members stop attending. What's keeping new members away and making members stop attending is an experience that isn't practical or connected to their day-to-day lives. When people are hungry, they tend to look for food, and many people order their food online. If you and your local church are not online, you are missing a vast sea of fish whom Jesus sent you out for. Right now three out of four Americans are on Facebook. If 75 percent of your community were located on one side of town, in one neighborhood, would you refuse to put a location there? I don't think so.

People don't want (or need) a rock concert or Starbucks; *they want (and need) to be discipled*. So what *is* discipleship anyway?

CHAPTER 2

Returning to Discipleship

When Jesus gave the disciples their last instructions before he ascended into heaven in Matthew 28:19, he made the mission of the Church quite clear. He said, "Now, therefore, stand and wait for people to come to your building on Sunday morning, then give them a great sermon to hold them over until the next Sunday." I'm sorry, what? What is that you say? That's not what your Bible says? Oh, you must have an old translation. The new translations say that pretty clearly. At least they must since that seems to be the way church is done nowadays. Local churches around the country have instituted the "weekend worship experience" model as a way to describe how intentionally they focus on making weekend church services the most exciting day of a person's week. This model includes light shows, free food, fun games, and exciting music. Many churches dedicate most of their staff and financial resources to making weekend services as close to perfect as possible, but there's one problem. Well, 360,000 problems to be precise.

Every year more than 360,000 people search Google using the search phrase "church online." That's thirty thousand people per month. If we break that down across four Sundays, that's 7,500 people every week. How many open seats would you have in your building if another 7,500 people decided to show up on Sunday? Is your pastoral team prepared to care for the needs of another thirty thousand people every month? These questions matter because, all jokes aside, Matthew 28:19–20 doesn't say, "Stand and wait for people to come to the building." It says, "*Go* and make disciples of all nations . . . teaching them to obey everything I have commanded" (emphasis mine). If thirty thousand people are *actively* searching for Jesus online every month, how many more need him *but aren't looking*? Facebook has almost 3 billion active monthly users, the vast majority of whom aren't searching for your Facebook page or the Facebook page of any church, for that matter. Yet research has shown that many of these people struggle with depression, suicidal thoughts, and feelings of isolation and helplessness.[7] These people need the hope of Jesus, but they aren't searching Google for "hope of Jesus" because they don't know he has answers. Imagine what would happen if instead of waiting for people to find us, we went out to find them? This is the foundational principle of discipleship: going *out* into the world to make followers of Christ.

Four key directives in Matthew 28:19–20 define biblical discipleship: *Go. Make Disciples. Teach. All Nations.*

If thirty thousand people are *actively* searching for Jesus online every month, how many more need him *but aren't looking?*

Go: The What

Many church leaders evaluate their effectiveness by how many people come to their building for weekend services—attendance. As a pastor myself, trust me, I get it. This makes a lot of sense because buildings cost money to operate, and you need to justify the expense against *something*. If people weren't coming to the building, it would make perfect sense to no longer rent a space or even to place a property up for sale. But instead of scrapping the attendance metric altogether, I wonder how much the approach to ministry would change if effectiveness were measured beyond the walls of the church too? What if effectiveness were also measured by how far the church community reaches *out* instead of only by how much the auditorium fills *up*?

Discipleship begins with the understanding that church isn't what happens at a building because the Church isn't a place. It's the global community of people who follow Christ and help others discover and follow Christ. As we seek to create a new benchmark, we don't have to look very far. Jesus is the perfect example of someone who went to meet people where they were. He didn't appear before the people only when crowds gathered on weekends at the temple. He didn't require people to meet him at a certain place and time before meeting their needs. He simply met needs as he encountered them. He was out among the Jews and gentiles alike, every day sharing the truth of God's Word and encouraging people to connect with one another around their shared faith. Jesus embodied *go* by never putting his name on any building, because he wanted to demonstrate through his life what ministry is all about: *movement toward others.*

Far too many local churches have simply become places people go (or not). But the power of the church is in being a community people belong to, whether or not they show up at the building we gather at every weekend. A return to discipleship requires us to reimagine our role in ministry so that we don't stop at waiting for people to find us before connecting with them. Discipleship compels us to *go* find *them.* Developing a social ministry mind-set begins with understanding that a vast harvest field of people in your local city and beyond are on social media but will never set foot in your building. But they are as in need of Jesus as the people you see every weekend. Our hearts must burn passionately for the souls of people we will never see in a pew because then we will finally internalize the meaning of *go* in the spirit in which Jesus commanded it.

What if effectiveness were also measured by how far the church community reaches *out* instead of only by how much the auditorium fills *up*?

Make Disciples: The Why

Knowing what to do is great, but at some point you need to know why you're doing it. In our case, after lacing up those digital walking shoes and heading out into the world of social media, you should be clear on why God is sending you. And let me dispel a couple of myths here. I've seen far too many Christians get into virtual shouting matches with other Christians and unbelievers alike relative to what the Bible says about any number of topics. These doctrinal battles tend to draw hard lines in the proverbial sand of discourse, but amazingly, I have yet to see one of these hundred-comment threads end with someone saying, "Thank you for this spirited debate. You have now changed my mind." Instead, the debates descend deeper and deeper into personal attacks and insults, slipping further and further away from the spirit of God's Word while people (amazingly) continue to quote Scripture verbatim. *This is not our why.*

No matter how astute your theology is, Jesus says it isn't your intellectual prowess that will convince people of your faith. It isn't even a perfect attendance record at church every weekend. The one thing that will reveal us as followers of Jesus Christ, according to him, is our love for one another (John 13:35). And loving one another begins with a concern for the souls of one another. When you love someone, you want them to see heaven, so your heart should yearn for chances to introduce Jesus to people who don't know him while helping them mature in their faith through discipleship. Jesus didn't ask us to follow him and leave it at that. He asked us to follow him and become fishers of people (Matthew 4:19), but he took it a step further in commissioning us to make disciples of those people.

I need to make an important distinction on this point. A lot of churches proudly tout "decisions for Christ" as a statistic, especially at year-end when reflecting on and recapping ministry activities from the year. This statistic indicates how many people reported praying the sinner's prayer and giving their life to the Lord during a service. Yet the question I always ask, and the question we should all ask, is, "What's next?" I'm avid about working out and being fit, and when I hear the term "decisions for Christ," I think about the people who sign up for new gym memberships right before New Year's. People get excited about the New Year and the opportunity to ring it in with a clean slate. They want to make it their best year ever. So a week or two before the New Year, they sign up for a membership at a local gym and commit to working out several times a week before or after work or school. They even go so far as to research healthy meal plans and exercise regimens with the goal of eating right, working out, and losing weight once and for all. While it's a noble decision, the data shows that more than 75 percent of people who make the decision to lose weight as a New Year's resolution don't follow through with it. All the energy, excitement, and emotion of the decision fade as the weeks go by. After being an avid runner and fitness enthusiast for the last seven years, I've learned to view the influx of extra people in the gym during the first couple of weeks of the year as a temporary inconvenience because the enthusiasm of their resolution inevitably and predictably dissipates within a few weeks. But their lack of

Discipleship is the process of a more mature, disciplined person coming alongside a less experienced, less disciplined person to help them achieve a **goal** they have set for themselves.

follow-through isn't for lack of desire. I believe it's for lack of discipleship.

The word *discipline* is derived from the word *disciple*. Discipleship is the process of a more mature, disciplined person coming alongside a less experienced, less disciplined person to help them achieve a goal they have set for themselves. While it's a word we primarily use in the church, it's applicable across contexts. If we return to the fitness example for a moment, discipleship would happen if a personal trainer put a new client through a specially designed workout to help them lose weight and build muscle. In addition to the exercise plan, trainers also tend to consult on nutrition to ensure their client gets the most out of the workouts because most people don't realize that fitness is 20 percent exercise and 80 percent diet. What makes a personal trainer so effective is not only the workouts or meal plans but also being a consistent presence and accountability partner to their client, a person who would much rather be at home eating chips and drinking soda while lying on the couch watching *The Simpsons*.

Ecclesiastes 4:9–10, 12 says,

> Two are better than one,
>> because they have a good return for their labor:
> If either of them falls down,
>> one can help the other up.
> But pity anyone who falls
>> and has no one to help them up. . . .
> Though one may be overpowered,
>> two can defend themselves.
> A cord of three strands is not quickly broken.

While a social media plan primarily focuses on sharing content to get likes, comments, and shares, a social ministry strategy focuses on building relationships and facilitating connections between and among people so that discipleship can happen. Relationships are the foundation for discipleship. And we don't build relationships on the weekends during the ninety-minute services we watch together, even if we are *together* in a building. More than a place to just connect with friends and family, social media is a digital mission field of opportunity for those who are willing to go.

Teach: The How

After consulting with countless churches over the last few years, I've noticed a common thread among their use of social media, regardless of size, denomination, or age. Their Facebook pages and Instagram galleries typically share information about upcoming events or pictures of lifted hands and worshipful faces from weekend services. You'll also see sermon graphics with catchy quotes from the pastor's latest message or video clips of the pastor preaching. What you *won't* see, however, is a lot of engagement with that content in the form of likes, comments, and shares. I've seen posts on pages with fifty thousand followers get thirty or forty likes and a handful of comments that mostly say, "Amen." The church communications teams would eagerly ask me, "How do we get more likes on our posts?" And if they were super savvy, they would ask, "How do we get the algorithm to favor our content and share it to more people?" Both of these are good questions. But they aren't the *right* questions.

More than getting additional likes and broader reach, the right question is: "How do we create an experience that facilitates connection with and among people?" You see, a

Relationships are the foundation for discipleship.

like is passive. I often "like" posts without reading the caption. Maybe the photo was cute or compelling. Maybe the first few words of the caption hinted at a wedding anniversary or other milestone event worth celebrating, so I click "like," or even "love." That in no way signifies that the content was meaningful to me, and if you asked me what the last five posts were that I liked, I couldn't tell you. But if you asked me about the last five Facebook conversations that interested me, I would do much better. I believe this is why Jesus didn't tell us just to *reach* nations; he told us to *teach* nations. Reaching is passive and doesn't require much effort beyond being seen. Teaching, however, requires capturing attention and fostering conversation. And those are much more challenging than simply sharing content and getting likes.

When Facebook's algorithm changed in 2018, there was a tremendous amount of weeping and gnashing of teeth from church communicators who were used to making a page post and seeing a healthy number of likes shortly thereafter. But what they didn't know is that many people had complained about how much the content from pages was clogging up their feed. After the groundswell became too loud to ignore, Facebook did formal research to better understand what was happening and what needed to change to improve people's experience on the platform. The research pointed loud and clear to one major finding: people want to spend time on Facebook when they are able to engage with content in a meaningful way. And that content needs to invite conversation, not just consumption.

People liked organization and brand pages because they

Discipleship doesn't happen by tossing biblical content at people.

liked what they stood for, in theory, but the content the pages shared wasn't interesting. It was a deluge of events, products, and fundraisers, but people preferred to see content from their family and friends because it was more relevant to their day-to-day lives. They were more likely to comment on, tag people in, and share those posts because they naturally sparked conversation. Many organizations and brands were upset by the algorithm change because they had been using Facebook as *broadcast* media instead of social media. In many ways, Facebook was just a marketing channel for one-way communication from the organization to the followers, but that was never the intent of social media. Social media should be social; it should invite multidirectional communication. It should invite conversation.

Conversation is fundamental to discipleship because discipleship doesn't happen by tossing biblical content at people. Discipleship is the product of dialogue about how to apply that content to people's lives in a way that leads to continual transformation. I'm not an educator by training, but one thing I know for sure is that *you can't learn by osmosis*. In other words, putting information into the atmosphere without any mechanism to help people understand it and make it practical to their lives doesn't facilitate its comprehension or application. This is why discipleship outside of weekend services is so critical. While we can teach people in a unidirectional way, it's most effective when we do it in conversation, when we create a feedback loop and allow for questions. Discipleship is the process of teaching people by coming alongside them, assessing their mode of learning, and meeting them where they are with the information they need in the way they receive it best. Teaching is more than sharing content; it's fostering understanding. Telling you that $100 \times 10 = 1,000$ doesn't become teaching until I help you understand how I arrived at that answer and also help you understand how to apply multiplication principles across other sets of numbers.

The Great Commission is about helping people learn God's truth so they can apply it to their lives. And learning isn't a passive experience. Romans 10:14 says, "How, then, can they call on the one they have not believed in? And how can they believe in the one of whom they have not heard? And how can they hear without someone preaching to them?" We learn best when we have a teacher to

Teaching is more than sharing content; it's fostering understanding.

promote understanding, which requires having a feedback loop where people feel safe enough to admit they don't have all the answers. The reason public pages have so little engagement is because that level of vulnerability isn't going to happen in a public space. More on this later.

All Nations: The Where

I had never gone on an international mission trip before October 2018. I had always wanted to but never had the opportunity. Yet even before traveling to Guyana, I had helped churches around the world build online communities in Africa, Australia, Germany, the United Kingdom, India, and South America. Before I ever left the United States to share the gospel in foreign lands, I had already helped share the good news in hundreds of countries, languages, and cultures because of the churches that were reaching their nations through social media. The message of God's faithfulness and Jesus's sacrifice was reaching the four corners of the earth digitally. And reaching all nations is what we have been called to do.

My husband and I together lead a local church in Gainesville, Florida, so I strongly believe in the important work done by real-life church communities in cities around the world. While the commission to teach all nations is often understood as *global* missions, I don't believe a local church fails the Great Commission if it doesn't go to another country on a mission trip. I do believe it fails, however, if it doesn't maximize the reach of its ministry to the furthest extent possible—even if the furthest extent possible is the end of the block. I have been to churches that have existed in their local communities for decades, but the people who live within a stone's throw of those churches don't know they're there. The members are perfectly comfortable with knowing who everyone is and often scoff at the few visitors who stumble in to check things out. The message is clear. We're not an "all nations" kind of church. We're more of an "all knowing" kind of church; we like to know all our members by name, so we don't do new ones. This mentality is a major reason why so many churches are dying. As members move away or die, the church eventually can't sustain itself and dies because there is no one to replace them.

Instead of being comfortable with the familiar fish in our aquarium, we can use social technology to swim out into the deep, unknown waters of the digital world to connect with people we would never meet otherwise. And this includes people in our local communities as well as beyond our cities' limits. People in your church, whether you have two members or two thousand, have relationships with those in your local community as well as in other cities, states, and countries. Some of those people know Jesus, but many of them don't. There are 2.3 billion Christians in a world of 8 billion people, so the math shows that the nations still need Jesus. Imagine what would happen if you intentionally built an online church campus in such a way that the people connected to your ministry connected with people they know and you were able to make disciples of those people by teaching them how to live out their faith daily? Now imagine what would happen if *those* people did the same thing and made disciples of others who made

> We can use social technology to **swim out** into the deep, unknown waters of the digital world to **connect with people** we would never meet otherwise.

disciples of others. What a powerful, unstoppable, and fruitful ministry you would have! And it's all possible. For free. More on this soon.

But It's Not Real

You may be thinking, "Yeah, Nona, I hear what you're saying, but real connections happen in real life, not online." This is a valid concern, and despite the many months we were unable to connect in person due to COVID-19, I think we can all agree that in-person, face-to-face, eyeball-to-eyeball ministry is essential. Some have suggested that the format for ministry is an either/or proposition, but I believe it's a both/and opportunity. We have spent many years and plenty of money perfecting our in-person ministry approach, but when the doors of our churches closed, too many of us were caught flat-footed because we thought we had to choose. If COVID-19 taught us anything, I believe it taught that we need to get equally good at building an approach for people who won't or can't come to the building but still need Jesus. The goal of social ministry is to leverage social media tools to build God's kingdom, whether in-person or not. I believe you will find that a strong digital ministry lends itself to the reward of driving online connections offline eventually. This is why discipleship requires conversation beyond content consumption. People are far more likely to visit a church where they have built relationships than one where they simply saw an advertisement. Online church is real church because it's filled with real people who need a real Savior. As long as we keep that in mind, we will be able to make use of social technology tools with the assurance that we are making a kingdom impact.

Now, before we go deeper into our exploration of digital discipleship, let's go over a quick primer on social media.

CHAPTER 3

Social Media Primer

Once upon a time, long ago in lands far away, people communicated ideas one letter at a time. Literally. Scholars, politicians, royalty, and priests translated their thoughts one letter at a time using ink and paper, two innovations that revolutionized communication long before the printing press, radio, television, or social media. The practice of writing one's thoughts for later recitation, review, or distribution changed the way we communicated. Prior to this, ideas were transmitted orally, with orators delivering their ideas in a stream of consciousness. The oral form of communication that dominated public discourse didn't allow for a suspension of time within which to reflect or process thoughts and ideas, but ink and paper provided that time and the opportunity for self-editing, curation, and the shaping of ideas before dissemination. Not only that, but the innovation of pen and paper facilitated the building of our first priceless set of recorded history. What had previously been only oral history became codified in words that could be read, translated, and distributed without the occasional literary license some took to make thoughts and ideas fit their own notions and worldviews.

Fast forward to today, and while we are the benefactors of incredible communication innovations, the landscape of social technology seems to have taken us forward while also taking us backward. What used to be the literal public square of ideas, a place where people gathered to sit and debate one another's thinking on a broad range of range of topics, has now become a digital public square of ideas, a place where everyone who has an opinion is throwing it into their friends' and followers' social feeds, stream-of-consciousness style. Whereas the public square of the past was constrained by whoever lived near the location and showed up to exchange thoughts on a given day, the digital public square has no physical boundaries and is not constrained by time. People from anywhere in the world can read a post at any time without missing the opportunity to interact with that content. People can now access an endless repository of content and catch up on whatever they missed. The public square now has a rewind option in case you missed it.

Merriam-Webster's Dictionary defines *social media* as "forms of electronic communication through which users

The public square now has a **rewind option** in case you missed it.

create online communities to share information, ideas, personal messages, and other content." That definition is pretty good but not quite nuanced enough for the contrast I need to make among the types of media we refer to as social media and what many of them actually are: internet-enabled broadcast platforms. To *broadcast* is "to send out or transmit something by means of radio or television or by streaming over the Internet." Holding these two definitions in mind, we will explore several of the most widely used "social" media platforms to determine which are social media and which are broadcast platforms with social *features*. Broadcast media exists primarily to deliver a message to an audience. Its communication style is unidirectional (one-way), and while there may be some limited interaction with the audience, broadcast media is passively consumed by individuals: watched, listened to, or read. Social media, however, exists to connect people to one another to foster a sense of community through conversation and engagement. It is intended to facilitate social interactions through content, as opposed to broadcast media, which is simply focused on delivering content to the highest possible number of consumers.

Having worked with all types of churches around the world, I have seen a standard set of digital platforms used, so we will review those with the caveat that new platforms are being created every day, so once you get this evaluation framework under your belt, you will be able to apply it to other emerging technologies to determine how they can and should fit within your social ministry strategy. Different platforms serve different purposes for different audiences, so we will review ministries' most commonly

Different **platforms** serve different purposes for different **audiences.**

used "social" platforms to understand each one's purpose, audience, and primary intended use, including YouTube, Instagram, Twitter, Snapchat, and Facebook.

YouTube

You will *seek* me and find me when you *seek* me with all your heart.

JEREMIAH 29:13, EMPHASIS MINE

YouTube was created on Valentine's Day 2005 and publicly launched nine months later to provide a video-sharing platform for everyday people. The first video ever uploaded was titled "Me at the zoo," and featured an eighteen-second clip of YouTube cofounder Jawed Karim at the San Francisco Zoo. As YouTube became more popular with amateur and professional video content creators alike—and amassed views by millions of people—it caught the attention of global search engine leader Google, and an offer to acquire the company was accepted for $1.65 billion. YouTube then became the video-sharing platform of the world's largest search engine.

Over the years, YouTube evolved from a place where amateur video content creators posted random videos of their day, to a place where "vlogging" (video blogging) became a thing. Content creators built substantial followings, and over time they were able to monetize their content through various deals with YouTube (i.e., Google) and other sponsors. As revenue opportunities became available through YouTube, video content creators became even more serious about their channel content, viewing it through the lens of their personal brand more than simply a hobby they did occasionally on the side. This professionalization of YouTube wasn't lost on Google, and as creators became more motivated to enhance their content quality, Google became more incentivized to apply its search-engine-optimization business model to their content as a reward for the best creators. Algorithmic distribution increased the probability that high-quality videos would appear in search results or be suggested as a next video to watch.

Since applying these changes, YouTube is now the world's second leading internet search engine, right behind its parent company, Google. While YouTube is still a video-sharing platform, its power is in its ability to categorize and organize videos in a way that offers precisely the content people are seeking. Most churches use YouTube as a secondary broadcast channel, often streaming their weekend worship services and special events. But without the context of YouTube being a search engine first, video-sharing platform second, churches aren't optimizing it as intended, which means the number of video views is probably suffering. How videos are titled and categorized is highly important because people use YouTube to learn how to do things or why things are done a certain way, so titling your sermon on forgiveness "December 31, 2019 Worship

Service" isn't going to pop up if someone searches "How do I forgive someone who hurt me?" Instead, title it as an answer to a question to get the best results.

YouTube has more than one billion monthly active users, but it doesn't facilitate connections between and among them or create communities where people can interact beyond commenting in threads beneath video content. Given this, YouTube does not reach the bar of "social" media, despite it widely being called that. It is a major digital media platform for sure, but YouTube's primary use is as a search engine for video content. Churches around the world began using YouTube heavily as COVID-19 became more widespread. While it proved reliable for sharing live video, it proved suboptimal for building a meaningful church experience after the video ended.

Instagram

God *saw* all that he had made, and it was very good.
And there was evening, and there was morning—
the sixth day.
GENESIS 1:31, EMPHASIS MINE

YouTube's primary use is as a **search engine** for video content.

In 2009 a marketing expert, Kevin Systrom, decided to start learning code at night to make a prototype for an app he wanted to build. The original idea for the app, called Burbn, was to let people check in at the places they visited. But after securing some seed funding to build the idea and joining forces with a partner to develop the app further, Kevin Systrom and Mike Krieger decided that instead of creating a competitive app to one that already existed, they would focus on building an experience that facilitated communication solely through photos. On October 6, 2010, after more than a year of development, Instagram launched. Within one week it had one hundred thousand users, and within two months it had one million. The app was so wildly successful that in 2012, less than two years after it launched, Facebook bought Instagram for $1 billion. As of 2019, Instagram has more than one billion active monthly users.

Instagram continues to focus product development on its original purpose of fostering communication through visual experiences. It remains a highly streamlined app, despite being owned by Facebook, a company that builds multiple platforms and content types within the Facebook app. Instagram continues to be a place where people experience life together through photos and videos, and research has shown that visual images are forty times more likely to be shared than text, which is why Instagram is such a widely used and popular app.[8] Despite Instagram's being acquired by Facebook, the founders and subsequent leaders of Instagram have fought against the mission creep inherent in working for an organization that lives in a constant state

The common thread driving churches' Instagram use is the goal of **maximizing** in-person **attendance** at upcoming events.

of beta—a constant state of experimenting, innovating, and designing. Instagram remains true to its beginnings as a photo-sharing platform, now enhanced by video opportunities through Instagram Stories (developed as direct competition to Snapchat), Instagram Live, and IGTV.

When you check the Instagram accounts of most churches, you tend to see photos from past events, programs, and gatherings, and you also see advertising for upcoming events. As with other digital media platforms, the common thread driving churches' Instagram use is the goal of maximizing in-person attendance at upcoming events. In other words, Instagram is being used as a free digital billboard with which to announce what happened and/or will be happening at a given church building. Since Instagram was created to be a place where images spark conversation and connection, limiting photos to those that capture events people may or may not have attended doesn't fully optimize what the platform was intended to do. Instagram's primary intended use is visual storytelling, which means posts should spark interest and conversation, not just consumption.

Even given this, however, Instagram's platform is not purely social because while it clearly fosters connections between users and *content*, it doesn't necessarily foster connections among *users*. In this way, Instagram is a hybrid of a social and broadcast platform, but it is more of a broadcast platform than a social one. There has been a surge in the use of IG Live since the advent of COVID-19, but without a space to have conversations afterward, it has proven to be a great platform for episodic video streaming, but not great for building community.

Twitter

A hot-tempered person stirs up *conflict*,
but the one who is patient calms a quarrel.
PROVERBS 15:18, EMPHASIS MINE

The story of Twitter's founding is riddled with questions, but the one thing widely understood to be true is that it launched in July 2006. Its original purpose was to provide a way to send short-form text messages to a group of friends, but Twitter has grown to be the world's largest online news-sharing platform. It crossed the 200 million–users mark in 2013 and had almost 350 million as of 2019. Although it is categorized as social media, it is primarily a digital broadcast service that uses "microblogging" as its communication mechanism. The original 140-character limit was selected because that was the character limit for text messages at the time. That constraint meant information was shared in quotable, condensed chunks. The text limit was doubled to 280 characters in 2017, but the average character tweet length remains unchanged at thirty-four characters.

Although all "social" media platforms have become mired in controversy at some point because of high-visibility conflicts among users and issues with fact-checking in cases of slander and defamation of character, Twitter has been most vulnerable to conflicts because of its primarily text-based nature, along with character limits. In defense of Twitter, I believe it has also become home to some incredibly thoughtful conversation threads *when used responsibly.*

While many churches and pastors use Twitter as a *micro-megaphone* to share Scripture and sermon quotes, one of the most powerful opportunities Twitter presents is the ability to engage in trending conversations and to use hashtags as a tool to insert a voice of hope, faith, and reason into conversations that would otherwise deteriorate into arguments. Twitter can be thought of as a "speed dating" site that allows you to quickly connect with users on the basis of trending topics or personality.

Twitter has the capacity for social connectivity if tweets invite responses and if dialogue is encouraged. The challenge, however, is that many churches and leaders "tweet and leave," citing being too busy to respond to comments or questions. My primary rule of social ministry is this: if you're too busy to engage, you're too busy to post. Twitter should be viewed as the place where conversation rules, all within 280 characters.

Many churches and pastors use Twitter as a *micro*megaphone to share Scripture and sermon quotes.

Snapchat

A cheerful heart is good medicine,
but a broken spirit saps a person's strength.
PROVERBS 17:22 NLT

Snapchat emerged onto the "social" scene in the summer of 2011 with the goal of helping people communicate in a lighthearted way through images and videos. While it initially sounds like Instagram, Snapchat took the digital space by storm because unlike Instagram, which stores posts indefinitely, Snapchat added a constraint that increased the urgency with which content was consumed: ephemerality. When a person shares a message (i.e., a "snap") with their followers, it gets deleted immediately after being viewed by a follower, and unopened snaps are deleted after thirty days. Specifically because of this feature, Snapchat became the digital communication platform of choice for gen Z. They enjoyed the ability to share images and videos without worrying about the content coming back to haunt them later in life. As an aside, this particular functionality has become of tremendous concern to parents who worry that their children will share risqué photos and videos assuming there will be no consequences.

Snapchat describes itself as a camera app rather than a social media app because it provides a wide and ever-changing range of photo filters and effects to enhance users' content. While many churches remain perplexed about how to use Snapchat, the ones that have embraced it have done so primarily to connect with a younger audience. Since Snapchat is a camera app, the best content has limited text but is visually striking and engaging. Churches that are successfully using Snapchat tend to use it for three purposes: support, awareness, and connection. Support tends to be offered by way of encouraging Scriptures to keep young people's minds focused on the goodness of God. Awareness is also important to keep youth up-to-date on events and gatherings where they can connect offline. Connection is fostered by spotlighting youth and celebrating the good things happening in their lives.

While Snapchat is widely viewed as a social media app, it is more of a broadcast platform that enables people to quickly consume fun visual content. As of 2019 Snapchat had slightly more than two hundred million daily active users, primarily in North America and Europe.

TikTok

I will build you up again,
    and you, Virgin Israel, will be rebuilt.
Again you will take up your timbrels
    and go out to dance with the joyful.
JEREMIAH 31:4

TikTok is a wildly popular video sharing app that originally launched in China in September 2016 under the name A.me. The app was rebranded as Douyin and grew to more than 100 million users within a year. The app's parent company, ByteDance, bought the app musical.ly to acquire the app's younger, US user base and consolidated into one app known as TikTok. The app was initially enjoyed by younger users, but it eventually caught on with users of all ages and has continued to grow in popularity.

Youth pastors have been particularly interested in TikTok as a way to engage with the youth they serve in creative, fun ways. Like other social platforms, however, there is no community component to TikTok that allows for relationship building beyond consumption and sharing of content. During COVID-19, TikTok became a source of entertainment for children and families who have sought relief from the anxiety and frustration of being quarantined.

Facebook Pages

How good and pleasant it is
        when God's people live together in unity!
PSALM 133:1

Facebook was launched as TheFacebook in 2004, beginning as a networking site for Harvard University students, then expanding to include other Ivy League schools. It eventually grew to include anyone with a college email address and by 2006 expanded to anyone age thirteen or older with a valid email address. The initial focus of TheFacebook was to connect people to their friends and family and provide a way to facilitate awareness about life events, but as the platform's popularity grew, the company introduced a feature called Newsfeed that allowed people to see a rolling list of updates from people they were connected to. As businesses and brands saw the growing user base of TheFacebook— eventually renamed Facebook—they clamored for the opportunity to have a presence on the platform. But Facebook required authentic human identity to use the platform, so brands and organizations were left out. Until Fan Pages.

In 2007 Facebook introduced Fan Pages as a chance for brands and organizations to share content with users who decided to become a fan of their page. By late 2007 more than one hundred thousand brands and organizations had pages. While Fan Pages were created to be the organizational equivalent to a personal profile, they don't have the same functionality and privacy settings as personal profiles. Whereas personal profiles can be private and not discoverable in a search, pages are, by default, public. Whereas personal profiles can send messages to friends and nonfriends through Facebook Messenger, pages can't initiate contact with followers through Messenger unless followers interact with them *first*. This important constraint was built in to prevent organizations from spamming users and has also become a point of contention for organizations that want to directly connect with page followers who may not see their posts.

The primary intended use for Fan Pages has historically been sharing information *about* the brand or organization it represents, acting as a digital billboard. To this end, most churches have used their page as a place to share information about upcoming events, quotes from sermons, and announcements. During COVID-19, Facebook Live on Pages became a

Facebook is the only truly social media platform.

major lever for keeping churches active while unable to gather in buildings, but a live-only strategy also revealed some limitations. For about ten years, Fan Pages received a healthy distribution ranking through the original algorithm (i.e., page followers usually saw the content posted to the page), but when Facebook's mission changed in 2017 to prioritize community building over content sharing, page owners were angered to learn that their posts' reach was significantly adversely affected. The new algorithm reduced the distribution of page posts, boosting distribution only on posts where there was heightened engagement via comments, likes, tags, and shares. Since many ministries did not aim for engagement on their pages, the new stipulations requiring multidirectional engagement between the organization and its followers, *as well as* among its followers, entirely changed the understanding of how best to leverage Facebook. Churches realized during COVID-19 that going live on their page, while a great tool to replicate their in-person weekend gatherings, limited their impact to episodic content, an experience that felt flat when compared with the many components of church life that extended beyond the weekend. More on the solution to this soon.

To qualify as a social platform, the platform must go beyond sharing information to facilitating multidirectional communication among and between users. With this qualification in mind, Facebook is the only truly social media platform. It is the place where people can connect with one another and build deep relationships fostered by social technology. While the other named digital platforms can share information, they don't go so far as to connect users to one another. This is why Facebook will form the basis for our social ministry shift.

CHAPTER 4

Why Facebook?

A whopping 2.7 billion people, more than a third of the earth's population, are active on Facebook every month. The platform with the next closest reach is Instagram, which is owned by Facebook. To get a sense for just how widespread Facebook is, if you're in the United States and asked your weekend service attendees how many of them are on Facebook, eight out of ten of them would raise their hands or lift their heads with a curious look on their faces because they were scrolling through Facebook and missed the question that prompted all the raised hands around them. It's widely believed that only older people are using Facebook nowadays, and it gets a bad rap in churches for not being used by millennials and gen Z, but the data tells an entirely different story.[5] People under age thirty-four make up 63 percent of Facebook users. While it is true that less than 6 percent of users are between thirteen and seventeen years old, that's still 162 million people—nothing to shrug your shoulders at for purposes of ministry.

People under age thirty-four make up **63 percent** of Facebook users.

Another 25 percent are eighteen to twenty-four years old, and 25 percent of 2.7 billion is 675 million people. That *one* slice of the Facebook universe is almost as large as the entirety of Instagram or YouTube. And it's growing.

But beyond the sheer number of users, why Facebook? Many churches invest in their own apps to house content and provide a mechanism to keep members and visitors aware of upcoming church events and other useful information, but pastors I have talked to have concerns regarding their church's app. First, the percentage of people who download the app is lower than they would like, and second, the percentage of people who use the app is even lower. They have an adoption problem and a usage problem. The app may be beautiful and rich with content, but it stops short of being a regular part of their members' lives, something Facebook already is. Whereas people open church apps only for specific reasons (e.g., to listen to a sermon, see upcoming events, etc.), the vast majority of Facebook users check it regularly throughout the day simply because it's on their phone and their phone is in their hand. They check Facebook while waiting in line at the grocery store, while sitting at dinner with friends, while at a stoplight. Facebook is already integrated into their daily lives.

Let's go back to an earlier statistic I shared. Right now eight out of ten Americans actively use Facebook. This is the exact inverse of the percentage of people attending a church service on the weekend: two in ten. If you knew that 80 percent of your community gathered every day in one place, wouldn't you strongly consider building a church there? Allow me to make a careful distinction. I'm not asking whether you would consider posting a *billboard* there; I'm asking whether you would consider building a *church* there. Having a Facebook page is great, but it's the digital equivalent of a billboard and, while it can serve as an entryway toward discipleship, the page by itself is not where discipleship happens, just as the auditorium is not where discipleship happens. Furthermore, church apps are great for housing content, but the Church is called to be more than a "house of content." We are called to be the light of the world (Matthew 5:14). Unfortunately, many churches are burying that light beneath the "bowl" of an app (Matthew

If you knew that **80 percent** of your community gathered every day in one place, wouldn't you strongly consider **building** a church there?

5:15) by storing their content in places where only members would know to look or even be interested in looking. While Christians may go to an app store to find tech that helps them grow spiritually, those who aren't yet Christians aren't scrolling through apps in search of Jesus. A church app is fantastic for people already connected to your church, but we are called to *go out* and be fishers of people (Matthew 4:19), not simply to serve the fish in our aquarium. We must keep our eyes on the horizon to reach the vast sea of people who are searching for an authentic experience with Jesus through an online church community.

Instead of swimming against the current of people's behavior patterns and preferences, we should strive, to the best of our ability, to integrate ministry into what's already a familiar experience. As a real-world example, instead of opening a coffee shop in the basement of your church that is open only on Sunday mornings during church services, what if you partnered with local Starbucks cafés to offer prayer to anyone interested from 7:00 a.m. to 9:00 a.m., Monday through Friday? What if instead of building a new offering or program that you hope attracts people to your church building, you gathered a group of church members and went to the places people frequent? Digitally, Facebook is where the people are. It's the Starbucks, while your church app is the coffee shop in the basement that's open on the weekends to the people who know it's there. When it comes to something as serious as sharing the gospel and transforming lives, if it ain't broke, don't fix it. Go where the people are, and integrate ministry into their routine.

Facebook is not only the largest, most frequently used

The Church is called to be more than a **"house of content."** We are called to be the light of the world.

social media platform, but it is also the only truly social media platform. Unlike YouTube, Instagram, Twitter, and Snapchat where you can follow people to watch their content, the algorithmic distinction Facebook makes is rooted in the company's goal to drive relationship building over content sharing. Content that has the most engagement is the content most likely to be seen by people because the algorithm views high engagement as correlated with personal interest, and personal interest is foundational to relationship building. In contrast to digital broadcast platforms that share information to a viewing, listening, or watching audience, Facebook allows (and encourages) organizations to facilitate connections and conversations between and among the people following them. But many churches use Facebook only to share content *about* their ministry (noun) and the page isn't the place where ministry (verb) *happens*. Ministry requires conversation and connection.

You should think about your Facebook presence like a house, where your page is your front porch. People can come up to that porch and see what you have there and passively learn a little about you. But people don't get to know one another on the front porch. You get to know people when they come inside your home and meet in your

Go where the people are, and **integrate ministry into their routine.**

living room. And a Facebook group can be the digital living room of an online church campus. Unlike other types of social media or church apps that are transactional at best, Facebook groups accomplish two key objectives necessary for ministry to take place:

1. The people are already on the platform (attendance).
2. The people can connect with one another (relationship).

A Facebook page, Twitter, Instagram, YouTube, and Snapchat are great for sharing content with the people following your accounts, but they can't and don't facilitate connections among your followers. In other words, people leave those platforms with new information, but not necessarily with new friendships. Some great church management systems purport to provide a community feature to connect congregations online, but you still have the dilemma of getting the people to download and adopt a new tool (difficult at best) and getting people to use it for the purpose you intended. The rate of adoption is low, and the rate of usage is even lower. This is why Facebook groups are the ultimate (infra)structure for an online church campus. The people are already there, so now it's just a question of leadership and digital discipleship systems. But before we get there, I want you to understand at a psychological level why this shift to social ministry matters. We all know there is a kingdom opportunity here, but let's be honest. While Facebook is a free platform, it will take resources to make this strategic and operational shift, so why do it? It's so much easier to schedule posts several weeks out and just let them auto-post. What's the big deal?

Social Media and Well-Being

Two are better than one,
>   because they have a good return for their
>   labor:
If either of them falls down,
>   one can help the other up.
But pity anyone who falls
>   and has no one to help them up.

ECCLESIASTES

A number of psychological studies have found a correlation between social media use and depression, leading a number of researchers to call for limiting it to no more than thirty minutes per day.[10] Yet if we dig into the data, we find that all social media use isn't created equal. *Passive* consumption of social media, such as aimlessly scrolling through timelines or watching other people's posts but never posting, is what adversely affects users. When we scroll through our newsfeeds, we will undoubtedly come across pictures from our friends out having dinner parties that we apparently weren't invited to. Or we will come across a post from a gym-obsessed friend bragging about their three-hour session, while we lie in bed eating chips and drinking soda. It's virtually guaranteed that we'll see a post from a holier-than-thou friend about her latest 120-day fast and how she touched the hem of Jesus's garment that morning, while we struggle to fit in five solid minutes of prayer every day. The issue with social media arises when it's used primarily to share content that people consume and compare their lives with. The research shows that social media becomes a powerful and positive resource when it's used to facilitate connections and build community. In other words, when social media fosters relationships, it becomes a valuable asset. That's when social media becomes social ministry.

Making It Real

The large ministry I had been working with for months was finally ready to launch an online campus for the people who tuned in to their livestream every week. They weren't initially interested in using Facebook groups for their local church community because they didn't think it was necessary. In their minds, they had all the bases covered when it came to ministering to their local congregation, but when we looked at the analytics of their Facebook Live viewing audience, we noticed people tuning in from other cities and states, I encouraged them to launch an online campus through Groups to connect with those people during the week and the church leadership agreed to give it a try.

I helped them develop the strategy to use a

Facebook group for their livestream viewing audience, and we launched it as their Facebook campus. As their Facebook campus grew past the ten thousand–member mark and people started feeling safe to open up, one parent after another posted in the group. They asked for prayer as they each sought help for their child addicted to opioids. Response threads grew to be hundreds of comments long as parents shared the struggles they had been privately battling. People were so moved by discovering they weren't alone that they self-organized prayer calls on that one issue to support each other.

When we witnessed what was happening in that Facebook campus, I suggested that the church create other Facebook groups linked to the main group where they could identify people with expertise in drug addiction to help lead that community. After a couple of days of planning, the linked group was created and publicized in the main group as a new gathering place dedicated to helping those dealing with opioid addiction. It had five hundred members by the end of the first day. The professionals who agreed to help lead it became trusted advisors to all the parents. And since the professionals were all Christians, they were able to provide biblical counsel in addition to their professional expertise.

The church's leaders had never considered the possibility that opioid addiction was touching their church, and not because they didn't care. The church was large, and the issue never rose to a high enough level to get their attention. After seeing the conversation and engagement in the Facebook campus for themselves, leaders decided to conduct a needs assessment for their *local* congregation and were floored to discover that the issue was just as prevalent. They prioritized building a resource team to help families confront and break drug addiction, and they opened the Facebook campus to their local congregation to give them 24-7 access to support.

Social ministry happens when we meet people's needs where they are, even if they never set foot in our buildings.

PART 2

The What

CHAPTER 5

Anatomy of a Facebook Campus

I stepped off the stage after speaking at a digital ministry conference of about two thousand pastors and church communicators in Charlotte, North Carolina, when an older gentleman with a twinkle in his eye approached me. After introducing himself, I learned he had been pastoring a large church of ten thousand members for the last twenty years and was excited about the prospect of digital ministry. He was especially excited to tell me about his online church.

"I saw the writing on the wall about five years ago. We were seeing fifteen thousand people every weekend across our different campuses, but that number dipped year after year until I had to close two of our satellite campuses. That's when I told my team we needed to get into online church."

"That's super perceptive of you. How is everything going?" I asked.

He smiled wide. "It's *really* thriving. We have more people watching us online than we have in our building. It's been incredible. Beyond my imagination."

"That's wonderful. So other than watching your service, what else does your online church offer?"

He just gave me a blank stare.

If you polled a group of pastors and asked them whether they did "church online," many would say yes—if they stream their *service* online. Somewhere along the way, church has become entirely defined as a building-centric, Sunday morning, ninety-minute production. It has become a place people go to watch a program, and because of that, churches are no longer just competing with other churches; they are competing with all the other entertainment options people have. Pastors have decried livestreaming as driving down attendance, but churches that have opted out of livestreaming aren't immune to the declining attendance trend. The idea that "If I livestream my service, they won't come" doesn't ring true, because church is not a program to watch; it's a community of people to belong to. When weekend attendance declines, it isn't simply because people are at home watching in their pajamas. It's because they are missing a human connection—a community—to keep them coming to the building. As a preacher, I completely believe in one unchanging gospel, and I *also* believe advances in communication tools provide evolving methods to share it. So why has our universal approach to "church" become so stuck in one mold? And why, when new technology provides the tools to break the mold, do we just reshape the mold on a digital platform? The reason so many pastors limit their online churches to livestreaming is because we have forgotten what church is: people.

From my vantage point, an online church and an offline church have something very important in common: they exist to minister to the lives of real people. The main difference is that an online church never closes; so whereas offline church may try to fit ministry into a ninety-minute box every weekend, online church has the capacity to minister to people's lives 168 hours per week. Every second. Every minute. Every hour. Every day. Every week. Every month. Every year. And because of this, your online church has to be built to transform lives. Life transformation doesn't happen by osmosis every Sunday, so why would we think it could happen that way online? A weekend worship service is constrained by physical space and time, but an online church isn't bound by those limitations. Instead of shaping an online church to fit offline constraints, you have the freedom to shape your online church around its only constraint: your vision.

Form + Function

Anatomy is the study of form, and physiology is the study of function. Form without function is lifeless; function without form is chaos. You need both to have an impact. Your online church should have a clear, compelling vision driving its creation to provide form to its existence. You may never shake the hands of the people in your Facebook campus, but they are just as real and just as worthy of ministry as the people who show up at your building. Because of this, your online church should be started on purpose, with purpose. Since you wouldn't haphazardly approach launching a new offline church campus, you should give as much thought and care to launching your online campus, with the following structural considerations: leadership, staffing, resourcing, timing, and geography. Let's take each of them individually.

LEADERSHIP

I have yet to meet a senior/lead pastor who launched a new physical location without a campus pastor and just hoped it would work out. While I've met countless amazing church communicators over the years, I've never met a senior/lead pastor who staffed a new physical location with a communications coordinator as the campus pastor. Yet when it comes to an online church, I routinely find communications and marketing staff being tasked with the goal of building it into a thriving community. But if you wouldn't make the communications coordinator your physical campus pastor, you shouldn't make them the one who leads your online campus, because different roles for different goals. Pastors lead and care for the people connected with their church. They are ultimately responsible for ensuring the spiritual growth and maturity of that congregation and the health of the church culture. Communications leaders, on the other hand, focus on creating and sharing content that compels people toward specific actions (e.g., attending service, registering for a conference, volunteering in the nursery). Both roles are compatible and necessary, but they are entirely different. Communicators go wide; pastors go deep.

While a successful Facebook campus does need communicators who can create compelling content that drives people's responses and behavior, it also needs a pastor who is committed to creating the necessary spiritual depth for people to grow. A successful Facebook campus requires identifying and appointing a pastor to lead people in the direction of maturity through discipleship. They would ideally be a salaried, full-time staff member because of the important role they will play in managing the campus and implementing a discipleship program. But if financial resources are limited, a leader who has the heart of a pastor and is willing to serve for kingdom rewards is equally valuable (more on this in chapter 6). We don't learn how to swim spiritually in the shallow end of easily digestible content; we learn how to swim in the deep end that challenges us to grow and learn. This requires going beyond posts with encouraging Scriptures to activities such as group Bible studies through Facebook Live or hosting small group meetups organized by neighborhood (more ideas in chapter 6).

STAFFING

After identifying the Facebook campus pastor, it's important to put in place a support team that has a passion for helping people deepen their faith online, a team not constrained by the idea that "real church" requires being in a building. This team should ideally reflect a cross section of the needs, demographics, and interests in your Facebook community. One of the easiest ways to determine these needs is by striving to create a digital counterpart to the real-life ministry teams serving your church. As examples, you should consider ministries for parents, women, men, youth, seniors, widows, the newly married, singles, etc. The options are endless, and you will notice that opportunities for ministry arise organically through conversations in the campus as you grow over time. The most important key here is to determine from the beginning not to leave the campus leadership solely on the shoulders of the campus pastor.

A campus support team is vital to ensuring that no one gets burned out. Unlike a real-life church building that has office hours and closing times, your Facebook campus will never close, so this becomes a great opportunity to leverage part-time staff or even staff paid with a stipend (e.g., $50 or $100/week). Support staff can also consist of people who have a heart to serve others for a heavenly compensation (i.e., *volunteers*). You can extend the reach and impact of your Facebook campus by casting a vision for your online church that helps raise up volunteers to supplement the work of your paid staff (if you have paid staff), but a word of caution here. While it may be tempting to "staff up" with volunteers, paying people is about more than the money. It's about what the money signifies. Fifty dollars per week could be all it takes to let people know that their service to your online church really matters to you and that you expect them to serve with excellence.

I strongly encourage you to appoint a support team that can relate to online church members and provide sound counsel. They should be people who "get it." An example I can offer is that of a mother with small children. When she posts in the Facebook group about being overwhelmed, it's great to have a children's ministry campus staffer ready to support and affirm her. The support staff should also be able to point her in the direction of some tangible resources. In other words, provide the same level of service you would offer should that same mother walk through your doors.

RESOURCING

An obvious benefit of a Facebook campus is that you don't have to budget for the rent, utilities, maintenance, and capital improvements inherent with a physical location. While the "hard costs" of a physical location aren't part of the equation, I would encourage you to resource a couple of "soft costs." Soft costs are essentially everything that isn't nailed to a foundation or housed in a building. For the purposes of your online church, I recommend investing in marketing, communications, and ministry teams.

I find it particularly interesting that in most churches the largest budgets are dedicated to the operations that help

We spend more money on the **fraction** of people sitting in our seats than the **mass** of people beyond our walls.

"maintain the aquarium" when we've been called to be fishers of people. We spend incredible sums of money on the building, instruments, lighting, church programs, and accounting systems—things that don't compel anyone to go out into the deep oceans of our communities to win souls. Instead, we spend more money on the fraction of people sitting in our seats than the mass of people beyond our walls. It's no wonder, then, that church attendance is plateauing or declining in two out of three churches in America. As the people we've catered to move or pass away, our church income inevitably declines, which means church leaders have to start making budget cuts, and without fail, the first place cuts get made is typically in the one area where growth is its central focus: marketing and communications (MarCom).

Although the words *marketing* and *communications* are often used interchangeably, they actually sit on opposite ends of the spectrum in terms of goals. Marketing is focused primarily on opportunities for growth. Its goal is to use data to better understand the ever-evolving, emerging needs driving a target population to choose (or not choose) you when they need your service. A good marketer will take it a step further. They'll uncover the psychological, emotional, and in our case, spiritual needs you must meet to help people see their need for you. The job of marketing is to help you stay ahead of trends so you can be the "market" leader in meeting the needs of your target population. Dying churches see their target population as the people in their pews. Thriving churches see their target population as everyone else.

Dying churches see their target population as the people in their pews. **Thriving** churches see their target population as everyone else.

Communications, on the other hand, focuses on facilitating information-sharing within an organization. While marketing focuses externally, communications focuses internally. The goal of communications is to maximize the probability that a message will be received as intended, so a communications team should think about which platforms and channels to use to share different types of content. The communications team should know about emerging technology and tools to help reach more people with a higher level of fidelity. In the case of communications, success is often measured by how many people received the content that was shared and took the action that was intended. As an example, if you have an upcoming conference, the communications team might develop an email campaign to facilitate registrations. Success might be the email open rate followed by the registration rate from email. Just as a campus pastor is necessary for leading a Facebook campus, marketing and communications are important to help it grow.

Marketing will help you understand the needs of people beyond your campus, while communications will help you reach them and connect them with your church.

After your MarCom budget, the next step is creating ministry teams to serve the needs, demographics, and interests of your Facebook campus. While your campus "address" will be a URL, the people you will serve live in physical locations and have physical needs. Your Facebook campus will serve as the global hub for your church, so people from all over will need local resources to grow in their faith. Imagine your physical church is located in Tampa, Florida, but your Facebook campus has people in Australia who want to do ministry there through your church. You would want to have someone assigned to help provide leadership and guidance to that ministry to ensure it stays healthy, right? The degree to which you resource your ministry teams should match the breadth of the vision you have for your Facebook campus. Your only constraint is the limit you place on that vision.

TIMING

Unlike a physical church, your Facebook campus will be open 24-7. Given the geographic diversity you will almost certainly experience, they may not even be in the same time zone. Thanks to the "always openness" of an online church, people won't have to wait for office hours to let someone know they need help. They won't have to wait until after service to corner a pastor and ask theological questions. You also won't have to wait until Sunday morning announcements to let people know important information. And you won't have to wait until Wednesday-night Bible study to share biblical truths. Everything that normally requires time and space for an in-person appeal or conversation will be immediately possible through a post from a mobile device. This means the timing of your Facebook campus operations will need to be dramatically different from that of your physical campus.

Your Facebook campus will need some level of leadership for most of the day, if not twenty-four hours per day. You won't need to have someone glued to their screen, but you will want to have coverage that ensures the campus is at least monitored periodically throughout the day to protect the health of the campus culture. We've all seen a single post create animosity, hostility, and division on our private news feed, so we want to protect against that. Monitoring the Facebook campus will also ensure that people who reach out for assistance get attended to in a timely fashion, which builds trust.

GEOGRAPHY

I mentioned earlier that you might have people in your Facebook campus who live in another time zone. The highly interconnected nature of Facebook means you will most likely have people from different cities, states, and countries joining your campus. Some churches use their Facebook group to build community for people who watch their livestream and not necessarily for the people who attend their physical location. In this case, their geographic demographics are extremely diverse. But even if your Facebook campus is used to deepen the impact of your ministry with your local congregation(s), you will find that the geography of your campus will extend beyond your local community. The reason is simple. Just as people invite

Just as people invite friends and family to attend a weekend worship service, people will **invite** friends and family to join your **Facebook campus.**

friends and family to attend a weekend worship service, people will invite friends and family to join your Facebook campus. In the case of your online church, however, they will no longer be limited by the physical constraint of distance from a building. Removing this physical constraint creates the momentum it takes to transition from a local church with local reach to a local church with global reach.

Make it a priority to stay aware of the geographic diversity in your group so that you can build a ministry infrastructure that meets people where they are. This could mean enhanced language capabilities. Or it could mean identifying and appointing support staff in other locations to facilitate in-person connections where there is a strong concentration of people. This is not necessary on day one, but it is a consideration you should keep in mind as your campus grows. Several of the churches I've worked with through the years have used the geographic distribution data in their Facebook group to plan for their next physical location expansion. The beauty of this is that instead of investing in a building and hoping people come, the people are already gathered online. The building simply becomes their new "offline" gathering place.

Recap

While it is true that you can create a Facebook group at any moment, the Bible cautions us to be thoughtful when it comes to what we do for the kingdom. Luke 14:28–30 says, "Suppose one of you wants to build a tower. Won't you first sit down and estimate the cost to see if you have enough money to complete it? For if you lay the foundation and aren't able to finish it, everyone who sees it will ridicule you, saying, 'This person began to build and wasn't able to finish.'"These structural considerations are designed to help you succeed from day one because we have only one chance to make a first impression. Leadership, staffing, resourcing, timing, and geography are the five pillars of a strong Facebook campus foundation, so take the time to work through each element to start and stay strong.

1. **Leadership:** Identify someone already on your team or within your congregation who has the heart of a pastor and a desire to extend the impact of your church beyond the physical boundaries of your community. You can also hire for this role.
2. **Staffing:** Identify people on your team or within your congregation who have a passion for ministering

to the needs of people and a heart for helping people grow even if they never meet them in person.

3. **Resourcing:** Commit to investing in marketing and communications to extend the reach of your church to people who may never show up at your building but who still need Jesus. Also commit to investing in ministry teams to meet the needs of the people in your online community.

4. **Timing:** Commit to meeting the needs of your Facebook campus across time zones and times of day by employing a team across shifts so the Facebook campus culture stays healthy.

5. **Geography:** Use Group Insights to understand where people are as your Facebook campus grows to identify opportunities to build ministry infrastructures in other locales, whether physical locations or satellite ministry teams. More on this in chapter 9.

Making It Real

The church had more than five thousand members when we first started working together, but their Facebook campus hadn't yet reached one thousand members despite the church having a Facebook page with ten thousand followers. When I met with the lead pastor to better understand how the Facebook campus was being used, I learned that it was mostly an afterthought. Someone had created it years before, but the church didn't officially associate with it. It wasn't much more than a digital coffee shop and wasn't considered an extension of the ministry.

After I engaged in a couple of months of meeting, visioning, and planning with him, the lead pastor realized there was more to the potential of the group than he thought. He appointed a team to explore the possibilities, and together we built a plan to make the group a strategic tool for ministry. He appointed a part-time online pastor to help rally a team around the online church and implement some intentional changes to how the group functioned. The online pastor engaged various ministry leaders in the group, and before long the group grew, and the level of engagement made the lead pastor say, "I would have never thought people would have such meaningful conversations online. It's really amazing to witness."

Within three months, the group grew 70 percent, and when the lead pastor saw the evolution, he decided to make the online pastor's role full-time and also invested resources in team members and the tools needed to lead the campus in discipleship. Today the group is a thriving, central part of the church and is often the first place people go when considering visiting a worship service.

CHAPTER 6

Planning Your Facebook Campus

As an executive and entrepreneur, I believe sustained success starts with a clearly defined vision by which opportunities are evaluated and from which decisions are made. To put it as Stephen Covey did in *The Seven Habits of Highly Effective People*, we should "begin with the end in mind."[11] My intent for this chapter is to help you think about the "end" you are trying to achieve as you launch (or relaunch) your online church. To build a thriving community, your goals and tactics should be aligned to best prepare you to build a successful Facebook campus from the start. I know it's tempting to jump into the "how" when you've made up your mind about what you want to do. But before you implement plans, you should first consider what you want to accomplish, and most important, how will you know whether you've succeeded? While it is true that Facebook is a free platform, you are still making an investment of time, talent, and energy that should yield a return for your church and God's kingdom.

There are a number of online platforms where you can virtually meet with your congregation, but Facebook is the only platform that has the necessary components of persistence and organization that will make the experience meaningful. For example, if you host a Zoom meeting, after you end the meeting, there is no mechanism for further conversation or connection. It doesn't have persistence. If you reach out to your members by text, the threads can become so long and cumbersome that important information gets lost. It doesn't have organization. Facebook is designed to help people connect after livestreams end and to keep content organized for later review.

Just as people launch local churches for different reasons, your online church could fulfill a purpose different from those of other online churches. Some people launch a local church as an outreach to specific areas of a city, while others launch a church to be a place for college students to explore faith. Some launch a local church to be a gathering place for the homeless and hungry, while others do so because they want to serve as a community hub for low-income families. Similarly, your online church could be the digital gathering place for your existing church members, or it could be a place for your livestream viewers who live in other cities, states, or countries. You could also create an online church out of necessity. I consulted with a church that had experienced a tremendous drop in attendance at its youth Bible study, so we created a youth Facebook group that allowed them to host their Bible study virtually.

Whereas fewer than ten youth attended the in-person Bible study, five hundred youth tuned in to the virtual Bible study in the Facebook group.

There's no *right* answer for the purpose of your Facebook campus, only *your* answer. And your answer matters a lot because other church leaders and colleagues will be looking to you to make the case for why the church should invest in something no one can put their hands on. But once you have your answer, the next step is to get buy-in from the key leaders and decision makers in your church. This part is crucial, and I have witnessed many ministries skip this step only to discover that people wanted to abandon the online campus a few months after it kicked off, because it didn't meet their expectations. Unfortunately, it's difficult to meet expectations that are never articulated, so before you get too far along in the planning process, invest some time into bringing people along.

"Just Another Thing?"

When you make the decision to launch a Facebook campus, people will undoubtedly say, "We don't have time to add another thing to our plates." Or they may say, "The communications team handles social media, so just see if they want to do it." The reason I provided the statistics around church attendance at the beginning of this book is because you will need to make a data-driven case at this juncture. Taking on another project usually requires displacing something else in a resource-constrained organization, so arming people with the case for online church is crucial to your success in getting

Regardless of how comfortable we are with **attending church** at our buildings, fewer and fewer people are coming to them.

buy-in where it counts. I have seen Facebook campuses at very large churches fail because there wasn't appropriate buy-in across the organization. Some people don't see a need for ministry beyond the four walls of a church, and I've watched them throw wet blankets on plans for a Facebook campus, so let's review the "why" again.

There are 350,000 churches in America, and two out of three of them are declining or plateauing in attendance. According to Gallup, 40 percent of Americans report attending a church service any given weekend, but actual attendance is closer to 20 percent. This means 80 percent of Americans are *not* attending a church service on any given weekend. Regardless of how comfortable we are with attending church at our buildings, fewer and fewer people are coming to them. And Google reports that each month more than thirty thousand people are searching using the phrase "church online." This means people are actively looking for church online while simultaneously not showing up in real life, so what may seem to be "attendance growth" for some churches is actually just "attendance decline" for others, as people simply move from one church to another.

Layer on top of this the new reality that, at any moment, the doors to your church building could be closed for any reason—global health emergency, natural disaster, and so on. If you stake your existence to a physical location alone, you will not only find yourself no longer viable, but you will also miss out on the vast sea of people who still need Jesus but won't look for him in a building down the street. While Jesus told us to become fishers of people, many churches have settled for being keepers of the aquarium. Our church buildings have become the fish tanks where the same fish keep swimming around. And while some new fish may jump into the tank every now and then, unless we fish in open waters, we will only poach from other churches' fish tanks. And no one wins. Especially not the kingdom.

Milestones

I will begin covering the technical aspects of launching a Facebook campus in the next chapter, but I want us to begin with the end in mind. As you will see in the following table, I recommend that you build your milestones backward from the target date of your Facebook campus launch to keep with the idea of "begin with the end in mind." The outline below covers a ninety-day planning period, but as we all learned from the COVID-19 pandemic, when time is of the essence, speed is necessary. You can shorten or lengthen your launch time in whatever ways you feel are appropriate for your church. If your church is ripe and ready for an online community launch, shorten it; if there are people who need extra convincing, lengthen it. Do whatever you need to do to plan for long-term success.

Goal(s)	Objective(s)	Target
Set date for campus launch and create Facebook Group	• Create the Facebook group and set group privacy to "private/hidden" to secure the preferred group URL while building out its infrastructure	90 days before launch
Establish campus purpose and vision and engage church leadership	• Create shared ownership and buy-in for the role of the campus within the broader church approach to community-building	80 days before launch
Establish Facebook campus leadership team	• Appoint a Facebook campus leadership team • Orient everyone to their roles	60 days before launch
Prepare Facebook campus for launch	• Link the Facebook group to the church's Facebook page(s) • Reorder tabs for group to rank first on landing page • Add group cover photo • Add group description/church information • Add group values/rules • Add upcoming events and other relevant information • Add curriculum for Facebook Units courses	30 days before launch
Group launch event	• Change group privacy to private/invisible • Drive mass in-person group joins	Day of launch

Campus Leadership Team

Your Facebook campus will succeed only if you have a strong leadership team in place. They'll need to understand their roles and embrace the opportunity to make disciples in a digital space. Your communications team may define their success by the number of views of your Sunday morning worship on Facebook Live. But your Facebook campus leadership team's success will be defined by how many of those viewers experience life-change through your church. As such, the following key roles should be filled to help you make the leap from social media to social ministry.

FACEBOOK CAMPUS PASTOR

- Lead and oversee the Facebook campus as an extension of the church's vision by reproducing the spiritual and cultural DNA of the church in the Facebook Group.
- Develop a vision and strategy to broaden the church's reach by impacting people of all ages, geographies, races, and life stages.
- Build a healthy campus leadership team by recruiting, appointing, and training staff and volunteer leaders to carry out the vision of the Facebook campus.
- Lead the campus leadership team to extend the reach of the Facebook campus by building teams of ministry volunteers to meet the needs of group members, regardless of location.
- Serve as a key member of the church leadership team by working with all church leaders to carry out the church's vision through various ministries, including children, youth, women, men, small groups, and more.
- Serve as the primary preacher/teacher for spiritual questions raised in the Facebook group.

FACEBOOK CAMPUS DIRECTOR

- Support the campus pastor by communicating and coordinating with all campus leaders and volunteers to ensure alignment of vision.
- Provide day-to-day operational management of the Facebook campus, including appointing new administrators and moderators.
- Identify, recruit, and train new volunteer leaders as needed.
- Prepare performance reports as needed for the campus pastor and/or senior/lead pastor.
- Ensure information shared in the Facebook campus keeps the group culture healthy and aligned with the overall church vision.

FACEBOOK CAMPUS MANAGER

- Support the campus pastor and campus director by managing communications within the group.
- Monitor the group for any issues that leadership may need to address.

Your Facebook campus will be meaningful to people only if they are compelled to engage with the content you post.

- Facilitate member engagement by serving as the first point of contact: welcoming them to the group, responding to posts, and flagging posts where additional follow-up from leadership is needed.

Engagement Calendar

Your Facebook campus will be meaningful to people only if they are compelled to engage with the content you post, activities you host, and other people in the community. The following seven-day engagement calendar provides some suggestions that can accomplish these three goals, and I encourage you to be creative in how you approach driving engagement. There are no rules for how best to do this, and you will begin to see common interests and questions emerge within the group that should further shape your tactics for engagement. The frequency with which you post and facilitate conversation should be based on the culture of your community. Some communities post and comment often, some less often. The goal, however, is to make it a meaningful place for people to connect with one another, your church, and their faith in God.

MONDAY

- *7:00 a.m.:* Bible verse of the day discussion question
- *12:00 p.m.:* Group poll: "What questions do you have about yesterday's sermon? Pastor [Name] will discuss here in the Group tonight at 7:00 p.m. EST!"
- *7:00 p.m.:* Monday Night Live with Pastor [Name] (discussing questions)

TUESDAY

- *7:00 a.m.*: Bible verse of the day discussion question
- *12:00 p.m.*: Post: "How can we pray for you today? [Name] will go live tonight at 7:00 p.m. to pray for and with you!"
- *7:00 p.m.*: Live prayer with [Name]

WEDNESDAY

- *7:00 a.m.*: Bible verse of the day discussion question
- *12:00 p.m.*: Welcome Wednesday (Welcome post for all new members)
- *7:00 p.m.*: Post new unit for upcoming sermon (more about Facebook Units in chapter 7)

THURSDAY

- *7:00 a.m.*: Bible verse of the day discussion question
- *12:00 p.m.*: Call to serve (ministry spotlight with opportunities to serve)
- *7:00 p.m.*: Thursday Night Live with ministry leader

FRIDAY

- *7:00 a.m.*: Bible verse of the day discussion question
- *12:00 p.m.*: Funny Friday post: "What's the funniest (G-rated) meme you've seen this week?"

SATURDAY

- *7:00 a.m.*: Bible verse of the day discussion question

SUNDAY
- Facebook Live weekend worship service(s) in Facebook group
- Facebook Live weekend worship service(s) on church Facebook page, with invitation to join Facebook group

Takeaways

Your Facebook campus will serve as your new church plant, and as such, its success will hinge on how well you plan for it *before* its launch. As with your offline church, your Facebook campus should be grounded by a clear vision that is not only held in your heart but is also captured and bought-into by the leaders serving with you to bring the gospel of Jesus Christ to your local church. As with any goal, it will only be as successful as the SMART objectives guiding your plan. SMART stands for specific, measurable, achievable, realistic, and time-bound.

- **Specific:** The milestones I provided are designed to help you move steadily toward a successful Facebook campus launch. While you can add specific milestones you believe will be needed for your church culture, I strongly recommend that you not skip any. The provided list has been created over time and honed from my personal lessons in helping dozens of churches launch Facebook campuses successfully— *and* unsuccessfully. The successful launches followed my provided road map, and the unsuccessful launches cut corners. Trust the framework.

- **Measurable:** As you complete each successive milestone, you should evaluate your readiness for launch. The plan is designed to take ninety days, but I have worked with churches that required less time and churches that required more. The ability to measure progress against milestones will be the key variable for a successful campus launch. This will be especially important as you identify and orient your Facebook campus leadership team.

- **Achievable:** Nothing succeeds like success. After getting buy-in from key leaders at your church, it will be important to show signs of momentum. The sample group rules, job descriptions, and engagement calendar provided in the next chapter are offered to help shorten your runway toward building that momentum, and the milestones are also important levers for demonstrating progress. And best of all, while launching a new physical location comes with the costs of rent or land or build-outs and more, launching your Facebook campus costs as much as a visit to Facebook.com.

- **Realistic:** Realistic plans effectively scope out the resources it will take to achieve the goal and the resources currently available. Since leadership is so critical to the success of your Facebook campus, I *strongly* recommend that you move only as fast as resources for campus leadership allow. In other words, if no one in your church (staff or volunteer) can serve as campus pastor, you should wait, watch, and pray until such a person is revealed. Everything hinges on leadership, so unless you are willing to launch a new physical location without a pastor, it isn't realistic to launch your online campus without one, which brings me to my last point.

- **Time-Bound:** Once you make the decision to plan for a Facebook campus launch, you need to draw a line in the sand and give yourself deadlines. Whether the planning takes ninety days, as I suggest, doesn't matter. You won't deal with the uncertainties that purchasing a physical property can create. That means the timeline from vision to launch is much shorter. Nevertheless, you should establish a timeline that honors the culture of your church and your ability to identify and orient a campus leadership team before launch. Successful plans are anchored to deadlines. Set them. Keep them.

CHAPTER 7

Building Your Facebook Campus

Think of your Facebook presence like your online house of worship where your page is your front porch, Live is opening your front door, Groups are your living room and kitchen, and Learning Units are your conversation starters. With those pieces in mind, it's time to build a fully integrated Facebook campus. You have created your page and you're using Live regularly to connect with your followers. You have put in the legwork to get buy-in for your online campus, and your launch plan has guided you toward making progress on your milestones. Your church leaders are on board with the vision, you've brought on a Facebook campus pastor, and you're ready to create your Facebook group. Now what?

Once you have the front porch (page) and front door (Live) working together, it's time to invite people inside your church by launching Groups. But there are so many tools and features within Facebook groups, so how do you make sure your group gets set up correctly? This chapter will help you set up your online campus for success from the beginning.

Getting Set Up

CREATING THE GROUP

The most significant and obvious first step toward building your Facebook campus is creating your Facebook group. You can create a group using the groups tab on Facebook or even through your Facebook page. You will be asked to name your group and provide some basic information, so I recommend naming the group something that is a natural extension of your offline church. If your church is named Faith Church, you might simply call it Faith Church Online or Faith Church Community. This is a crucial step, and many churches have gotten this wrong in an effort to be creative. The goal here is not to be creative; the goal is to be clear. Remember, you are launching an online church that will be filled with real people who have offline lives. Treat this with as much care and thought as you would treat launching a new physical location.

PRIVACY SETTING

You will be asked during the group creation process to choose a privacy setting: public or private. A public group is like a page in that anyone can see who is in the group and what is posted. All the content and activities of the group are visible to anyone who finds the group, but they will have to join the group to post content or comment in the group. Public groups tend to have low engagement, similar to that of a page, because people don't feel as safe to comment when they know anyone can see their posts. A private group, on the other hand, is discoverable in a search, but its contents and activities are visible only to group members. When a person comes across a private group, they are able to review the group description, privacy setting, when the group was created, and who the administrators are, but they have to request to join the group (and be approved) to see content and participate in conversations. If you make your group private, you will have the option to make the group visible or hidden. This setting determines whether your private group can be found by anyone, or whether only members (and those invited to join) can find it. For purposes of constructing your community, I recommend setting its privacy to private and hidden so you don't have to worry about it being discovered while it's under construction. Once the group is ready for launch, you will change the setting to private and visible. More on that later.

GROUP DESCRIPTION

You will be asked to provide a group description during the group creation process, and this will be an important opportunity to articulate why people should join the group. The group description will be the first thing people see when they visit it from search results or from your page (more on this soon), so it should provide enough information to let people know what the group wants to accomplish and why they should consider joining. A word of caution: make your description as inclusive as possible. If you say, "This group is for members of X church," that will automatically eliminate anyone who isn't a member, so instead, try to make the description expansive and broad so that people not connected with your church can see themselves potentially enjoying your community.

View the group description as an opportunity to invite people into the vision of your church and, more specifically, the vision of your Facebook campus. The description should answer the questions "Who are we?" "What do we offer you?" and "How can you engage here?" People join groups because they want to find solutions to problems they are facing in their lives, so focus on WIIFM: What's in it for me? Providing this information before people request to join will ensure that people who join the group have a basic understanding of what it's about. And that goes a long way toward establishing and maintaining a healthy culture.

Sample Group Description

Feel free to use and tweak the sample verbiage below for your group description. It contains the main elements needed to answer the typical questions people have before joining a community:

> Welcome to the [insert name] Facebook campus! This community was created to connect, support, and celebrate the members and friends connected with our church. This community is led by Pastor [insert name], who serves as the "on-site" leader for any needs you may have. They serve alongside a campus leadership team to make sure your experience here is rewarding. The campus leadership team is [insert names], and they are

all here to ensure this community lives up to the vision and values of our church.

We actively moderate this community [insert days/times], so if you need us, just tag us in a post, and we will respond as soon as possible. We are so glad you are part of our Facebook campus, and while you're here, we encourage you to:

- Share uplifting stories with your fellow community members.
- Seek advice, support, and prayer for the challenges you encounter in life.
- Celebrate the good things happening in your life and the lives of your family and friends.
- Ask questions about your faith or church happenings.

COVER PHOTO

Your cover photo will be the visual representation of your Facebook campus, so choose one that effectively communicates the culture you want to create and the vision you have for your online campus. If the vision of your Facebook campus is to be a gathering space for people of all ages, cultures, and nations, you should choose a cover photo that depicts the type of diversity you want in the group. If you choose to link additional groups to your main Facebook group (discussed further on page 104), you should use cover photos that appropriately illustrate the target audience for each of those groups while ensuring that the look and feel of each group is consistent with your brand. You can achieve this by using different images but including the church logo. As an example, a linked group for families caring for children with special needs should have a cover photo depicting children with special needs, with your church logo somewhere in the image and in the group name. It will be important that the groups look as though they are part of one organization. Otherwise people get confused.

In the two examples I just provided, you will notice that I'm suggesting you depict *the people* you wish to serve, *not your latest teaching series*. It can be tempting to replicate images from your page to your group(s), but you should always remember the different purposes they serve. A page cover photo detailing your latest teaching series may be a great way to heighten awareness to the audience on that page, but since your Facebook group is meant to be a gathering place for people to have conversations, not a container to gather people around episodic teaching events, the cover photo should be people focused, not marketing focused. I've worked with many churches that simply replicate the cover photos they use on their page for their groups, and it routinely creates confusion because both entities look alike. Keeping the imagery focused on people is the easiest way to set the expectation that the group is *for, by, and about them*.

GROUP RULES TEMPLATE

Just as in real life, essential ground rules will help your online church community function well. Keep your Facebook campus culture healthy by explicitly stating what type of behavior you expect (and will not allow) from the members. During the group creation process, you will be given the opportunity to establish group rules, and I highly recommend you do. You can add a maximum of ten rules, but I recommend selecting no more than three. There is a library of preset rules you can choose from, or you can create your own. The following verbiage is provided as an example, so you can use as much or as little of it as is helpful to you in setting the right tone for your campus.

The health of our Facebook campus culture is critically important to all of us, and we need your help to keep it positive. Please:

- Participate in a kind and collaborative way, and exercise respect and consideration while here.
- Avoid making any posts or comments that could offend a brother or sister.
- Avoid private messaging other members to demean, harass, or be unkind.
- Respect the privacy of other members of the group, and refrain from sharing screenshots outside the group.

Should we find that you are not adhering to these values, we reserve the right to remove you from the group. So please help us keep our culture healthy. Thank you.

Your Toolbox

Now that the basics are out of the way, I want to provide you with a primer on some of the important tools available in Facebook groups to help you create an experience that meets people's needs. One caveat to note is that Facebook is constantly evolving the Facebook Groups product to better serve users by incorporating feedback from group members and leaders, so while I'm providing an overview of many of the most relevant features for churches, this list will not be exhaustive because the product changes regularly. The features described below aren't in any particular order, so this overview will simply orient you to the capabilities of a Facebook group. *In the next chapter, I'll cover how to use these features for ministry.*

Group Type: The group type acts as a classification system that allows people to discover your group if they are searching for a specific category of group to join. In some cases, your group type selection also has the added benefit of unlocking specific group features. I suggest classifying your group type as "social learning" because that classification unlocks a feature called *learning units* that allows you to organize posts into a unit or series of units whereby you can integrate structured learning content into the group—also known as discipleship. More on this later.

Admin Tools and Insights: This tool acts as the management hub for your group. It's where people who have administrator access can take necessary action. This could include approving/rejecting member requests, changing the group type, changing the group description, adding/removing administrators and moderators, adding/removing membership questions, changing the group name, changing the group URL, and much more.

Post Scheduler: Administrators can create and schedule posts in the composer that will be pushed to your group on the date and time you choose. This becomes especially helpful as you implement the recommended engagement calendar. You will be able to schedule posts for the week in one sitting and not have to remember, for example, to make a post at noon every Wednesday. Distractions are inevitable in our daily lives, and I can attest that it's easy to go days without posting before realizing you've been quiet.

Announcements: As an administrator, you will also be able to designate posts for high visibility in the group. When a post is marked as an announcement, it becomes "pinned" to the top of the group, under the category "announcements." People will immediately see that there are announcements to read once they enter the group. You can even schedule announcements so that they are automatically removed from the announcements hub at a date and time you choose.

Personalization: Most churches have a brand identity that derives from a specific color palette. A key feature of your group is the ability to choose a group color that best aligns with your brand palette. The color will replace the standard Facebook blue and will give people the feeling they are "inside" your church.

Linked Groups: You can create a "network" of Facebook campuses and ministries by creating and linking groups to one another *and* to your page. I recommend having your principle Facebook campus group linked to your main church page. If you think it would be helpful, create and link ministry groups within your principle Facebook campus group. The ministry groups reflect the various segments of people you're serving (e.g., parents, men, women, youth). If you have multiple physical locations, I recommend having one page for your main church location, then build Facebook campus groups for each satellite location, and link them to your main church location page.

Polls: As your group grows, you will want to use structured mechanisms to evaluate its effectiveness and solicit feedback. Polls are a great way to do that because you can generate a poll in the composer and gather real-time feedback from your group members. You may be thinking about making changes to the group or you're simply interested in hearing about people's experience in the group. Either way, a poll is a great way to engage people and let them know you care about their perspectives.

Live: Facebook Live is one of the most popular products on Facebook, and it's no different when it comes to groups. Going live in a group, if harnessed the right way, has the added benefit of building a sense of accessibility between group members and church leaders. Whether your church is one hundred people or ten thousand, it's often difficult to connect with your congregants in a way that humanizes them. Going live allows you to lower barriers between you and your congregation and followers through the tap of a screen on your mobile device.

Membership Questions: This feature was born out of an effort to help group leaders get to know those joining their group. You can choose up to ten questions to ask a prospective member as they submit a request to join your group. Still, I suggest asking no more than three, to lower the probability that the person will get overwhelmed and leave the process prematurely. The questions should be relevant to your group's purpose. So unless your group is for painters, asking the person's favorite color will most likely just confuse them. For purposes of ministry, it makes sense to ask questions such as:

1. Do you attend one of our local [insert church name] campuses?
2. What would you like to get out of joining [insert online campus name]?
3. Do you know Jesus as Lord, or are you interested in learning about him?

Making It Real

I started working with a pastor of a ten thousand–member church who was interested in launching a Facebook campus for their regular attendees and the people viewing their livestream each week. While I was meeting with him and his team to discuss how to structure the campus, the youth pastor asked whether there was a way to sync Instagram and Snapchat with the group to connect with their youth. "Young people aren't using Facebook," was his rationale. I asked him to tell me more about what he wanted to accomplish, and he mentioned being discouraged by low attendance at their weekly youth Bible studies. "We used to have at least fifty kids a week, but now it's down to maybe eight. We can't compete with extracurricular activities. This generation just doesn't see church as important anymore."

I suggested that the church create a linked group exclusively for their youth and try hosting the Bible study as a Facebook Live event in the group after advertising it on the main church page. The youth pastor was skeptical, but he announced to the youth that he would host the next week's teen Bible study in a new Facebook group exclusively for them, fully expecting no one to join the group or to tune in. What happened next astounded him. More than 170 youth joined the group right after his announcement, and several hundred more joined over the course of the week. By the time the youth pastor went live, he had five hundred youth tuned in, watching and asking questions. After the Bible study ended, youth who were normally quiet in person were some of the most active commenters in the group.

What he initially thought of as youth not thinking church was important was actually just an issue of barriers: time, travel, and energy. Facebook removed all those barriers and provided a pathway for the youth to build community around their faith—right at their fingertips.

Takeaway

I talk to so many leaders who are overwhelmed and intimidated by social technology. They feel that the quantity of tools and the frequency with which the tools change is too difficult to keep up with, and this is why I wanted to take some time to help you understand what the tools are and how they can best be used for purposes of ministry. But even I know that understanding what the tools *are* is not the same as leveraging the tools *for ministry*. I plan to spend quite some time on that, but before you can use a tool to build something, you need to familiarize yourself with its purpose and function. My request and recommendation at this juncture of our journey together is that you take some time to use the tools while your group is in the private, hidden privacy setting so you can hit the ground strong when it comes time to launch the group, which is our next step.

PART 3

The
How

CHAPTER 8

Launching Your Facebook Campus

Once you've created your Facebook group and set it up in anticipation of soon letting the world know you're making the leap from social media to social ministry, you're about ready to launch! While your Facebook campus will differ from your physical church location(s), one of the advantages of launching a Facebook campus is the ability to get up and running quickly. Launching a physical church usually requires years of planning and saving, followed by months of advertising to let people in the area know the church is coming. But launching a Facebook campus requires only a few strategic promotions to get people to join and invite their friends. Since people are already on Facebook and are maybe also connected to your page, letting them know your Facebook campus is coming doesn't require more than a few weeks' notice. In fact, I've found that too much lead time can make people anxious because they're already on Facebook and want to join the group as soon as they hear about it.

While you won't need a lot of lead time for your launch, you *will* need a lot of excitement because Facebook can be a noisy place with a ton of distractions. Even beyond Facebook however, the people in your congregation need to know your campus launch *is not just another thing.* They need to know it's a new approach to kingdom-building, and because of that, it's ministry. After spending at least two months preparing to launch your new campus, you will want to get the actual launch right, so take the time to make sure people are crystal clear on the purpose it will serve in advancing your church mission and vision. You won't need to go door-to-door to tell people about it, as you might do for a new physical location, but you *should* use all the communication tools at your disposal to communicate the highest level of enthusiasm you can. Share your passion for the opportunity your new Facebook campus will provide for you and the people connected to your church.

I get asked a lot of questions about starting a new Facebook campus, as you can probably imagine, but the question I get asked the most is, "How do you get it to grow?" Thankfully, the answer is quite simple. You grow your Facebook campus the same way you grow your real-life campus: tell people it's there. *Constantly.* This is where your marketing and communications teams will be indispensable. In my experience, Facebook campuses that start off with a bang and then fizzle are the ones where people are invited to join on launch day but never hear it mentioned again. People join it on launch day, but it becomes

You grow your Facebook campus the same way you grow your real-life campus: **tell people it's there.**

"just another thing," nothing more than background noise in their already crowded newsfeed. This is why having a campus leadership team is *so* important. If you build excitement on launch day, then people join the Facebook group and find it inactive and irrelevant, they won't return to it and certainly won't invite their friends. You have only one chance to make a first impression, so launch day should be the "grand opening" that sets the bar for what people can expect in your Facebook campus.

Facebook Campus Launch Blueprint

After launching dozens of Facebook campuses with churches around the country, I see one thing that remains consistently true: successfully launching your Facebook campus will accelerate its growth and build enthusiasm within your church. I've worked with churches that have taken various approaches to launching their Facebook campus, from simply launching it without saying anything, to launching it and promoting it on their page, to launching it with flare during all weekend services. I have found the most successful tactic to be a formal Facebook campus

Churches have the unique advantage of **weekly touchpoints** with their members and followers.

launch event. Unlike other types of organizations that don't usually see the people they serve at a regular cadence, churches have the unique advantage of weekly touchpoints with their members and followers. This means you have a higher probability of driving the behavior you hope to see because you can capitalize on your time in front of people. While you could host a stand-alone launch event apart from your weekend service(s), I've seen the most success come from incorporating the launch event into the worship service(s) since that's where you have the highest visibility.

As with anything worth doing, you should have a plan to guide your actions for the event, and I recommend that your launch event plan clarify the following logistical and tactical considerations:

Date: I *strongly* suggest holding your campus launch event during your weekend worship service. If you have multiple services, hold it during *all* services. This will ensure that you maximize the number of people who join the group that day. I've witnessed events of all types and on different days of the week, and launching during your weekend service(s) is by far the most likely to set you up for immediate group growth and high engagement. There is nothing worse than being one of ten people to join a group and no one says anything. Pick the date with the highest probability of attendance.

Location: If you have multiple physical locations, I suggest holding your launch event at *all* locations to maximize the number of people who join the group that day. People are familiar with your church location(s), so don't host the event somewhere else. If people can't find where the event is located, they will simply go home. Make it easy for them.

Promotion: I outline a promotion plan in the next section of this chapter, and as always, you can tailor it to meet your own needs and resources. One piece of collateral that has worked well during launch events I have hosted is providing a flyer or postcard on the day of the event that outlines instructions on how to find and join your new Facebook campus. This flyer or postcard should match the instructions you share on your page the day of the launch.

Attire: Since the launch will be a special event, designing shirts for the occasion is a good idea. They should both pique interest in the event and build excitement for the new campus. I've hosted launch events where all volunteers and staff wore blue Facebook shirts and jeans the day of the launch as a means of raising awareness. You could design special shirts for your launch event with the name of your Facebook campus or a catchy phrase that points people to the new online church.

Swag: You can't have a party without giveaways, right? Your Facebook campus launch event presents a great opportunity to make people feel as though they're part of a special day. A few items that have worked well for other churches are church fans, T-shirts, sunglasses, and custom candy. You can have these items created locally, or you can order them online.

Tech: It's a good idea to have a few internet-enabled computer stations or tablets available in the church lobby. People may have a hard time signing up for the group on their phones or if they—*gasp*—don't have a smartphone. In some cases, you may even have to help people sign up for Facebook before they can join the group. It's a good idea to make sure all your event-day volunteers can help people on their devices, both iOS and Android.

Decor: Add a few inexpensive aesthetic elements that signal something special is happening. I recommend setting up a ten-by-ten-foot step and repeat (a photographic backdrop that people can take pictures in front of) with your church logo for photography purposes. People will post those pictures in your new group as a way to commemorate the day and capture the excitement. It's a *great* way to catalyze momentum from the beginning. You should also ensure that any digital announcement boards or TV monitors display graphics announcing the Facebook campus launch. And you can invest in yard signs and handheld signs welcoming people to the event. Balloons are also a fun and inexpensive option, but be sensitive to the fact that some people have latex allergies, so Mylar balloons would be your safest bet.

Teams: You will need three teams for your launch event: greeters, communications, and tech support. Your greeters are the people who will make everyone feel welcome to the event. Your communications team will help capture pictures of the event and post pictures and stories after the fact. Tech support are the people who will provide hands-on, one-on-one assistance to people who need help connecting to your group. It will be important to have all three teams in place to ensure no one gets trapped into helping someone on their phone while people walk by feeling unnoticed or taking pictures when people need help joining the group.

- Before Service
  - Greeters: Welcome people to Facebook campus launch day, and give everyone a church fan or another swag item as they enter the auditorium.
  - Tech Support: Ensure all computer stations/ kiosks are online and bookmarked at the church's Facebook group for easy login by attendees after the service.
  - Communications: Have a photographer on hand to take pictures of people in front of the

step and repeat, and also have a staff member
or volunteer posting about the launch in real
time across all social media platforms.

- ◉ After Service
  - ▪ <u>Greeters</u>: Thank people for coming, and give
    everyone a thank-you gift as they leave.
  - ▪ <u>Tech Support</u>: Assist people with getting
    connected to the group as needed (whether on
    their handheld device or at a computer station).
  - ▪ <u>Communications</u>: Have a photographer on
    hand to take pictures of people in front of the
    step and repeat, and also have a staff member
    or volunteer posting about the launch in real
    time across all social media platforms.

Promotional Blueprint

The following plan outlines a three-phase approach to promoting your new Facebook campus for thirty days prior to
the launch. It highlights important opportunities to keep
the Facebook campus top of mind after the event. These
are suggestions I have honed through coordinating dozens
of launches, so make them your own and be as creative and
fun as you like.

PRELAUNCH
- • "Facebook campus coming soon" promotion on
  Facebook page(s)
  - ◉ 4 weeks out: 2 times per week
  - ◉ 3 weeks out: 3 times per week

- ◉ 2 weeks out: 4 times per week
- ◉ 1 week out: daily
- ◉ Day before: Facebook Live with pastor inviting people to attend the launch event at the church and via livestream.
- 3 weeks out: Create Facebook campus launch event on page, and invite friends to attend.
- 2 weeks out *and* a week before: Pastor announces the upcoming Facebook campus launch live during weekend worship services.
- 2 weeks out: Change page cover photo to launch event announcement.
- 2 weeks out: Include launch event announcement in a weekly printed bulletin.
- 2 weeks out: Include launch event announcement in weekly video or live announcements.
- 2 weeks out: Add launch event to church website calendar and church website graphics.
- 3 days out: "Facebook campus launch this Sunday" video promotion on page
- Day before: Link group(s) to the church page, and change privacy setting to visible. *Don't forget this step!*

LAUNCH DAY

- Livestream all weekend worship services through Facebook Live on your page and in your group.
- Distribute "Join our Facebook campus" flyers/postcards as people enter the building.
- Pastor makes "call to action" appeal to join new Facebook campus (sample script provided below).

- Pastor publicly introduces the Facebook campus pastor and acknowledges campus leadership team.
- Administrators and moderators approve join requests in real time.

POSTLAUNCH
- Friday after launch: On your Facebook page, celebrate the number of people who joined your Facebook campus the week of the launch and include a link to join
- Promote campus on Facebook page
  - 1 week after event: daily
  - 2 weeks after event: 4 times per week
  - 3 weeks after event: 3 times per week
  - 4 weeks after event: 2 times per week
- Pastor or service host includes an invitation to join the church Facebook campus as part of the weekly welcome message
- Advertise Facebook campus in church publications/newsletters

Pastoral Call-to-Action Script

I have found that *nothing* makes a bigger difference in compelling people to join a Facebook campus than having the senior/lead pastor make the invitation to join it. When the pastor lifts their voice to say, "This is important," then people believe it. I wrote the following script and have watched countless pastors use it to aid their appeal, and I'm confident it will help you appropriately frame the "why,"

Nothing makes a bigger difference in compelling people to join a Facebook campus than having the **senior/lead pastor** make the invitation to join it.

"what," and "how" for successfully launching your campus. As always, feel free to make it your own while staying true to the structure provided. And please remember, this is intended to be said live by the pastor from the platform, not in a video or post.

- **The Why:** "In my years of pastoring, I've seen people come and go, and I've come to discover that the answer to one question determines whether someone will stay. The question is this: 'Are you connected to our church community?' God told Adam that it isn't good for man to be alone. Notice, he didn't say it's impossible; he just said it isn't good. And the Hebrew word that is translated to *good* really means 'best.' We will never experience God's best for us by doing life alone, because God created us to do life together in community. If you miss Sunday morning worship or your weekly small group, you can begin to feel disconnected from our church. Most people equate being a member of a church with attending events at a church building. But our church is not this building. This building is simply the place where our church *gathers*; our church is the community of people who are connected to our purpose . . . *and* to each other."
- **The What:** "It's our goal to build a church where you can always access the support you need to grow spiritually and face life's challenges with your

church family by your side. So today I'm excited to announce that we are launching a new Facebook campus so you can always stay connected to one another and our leaders. Even more, our new campus will allow you to invite your friends, family, and coworkers to connect with our ministry in a way that meets them where they are. It's going to be an important companion to our physical gatherings because even if you can't attend worship or an event, you can still be present with us as your church family."

- **The How:** "So here's what I want you to do for me. Take out your internet-enabled device—cell phone, tablet, whatever you have. Now visit our Facebook page [*put visual with web address/page name on the screen*]. From there, simply click the 'visit group' button and request to join our group. When you join, you will find yourself connected to our church in an even deeper way. I'm thrilled to announce today that Pastor [Name] will be leading our Facebook campus and ensuring that the community stays healthy and growing in faith together. If you need help, just stop and see one of our volunteers in the lobby as you leave today. I want everyone to get connected, so once you join, please invite a friend or two to join as well. Let's thank God in advance for what he's going to do through our new online Facebook campus."

Making It Real

One of the churches I worked with early on already had a Facebook group when we first met. Still, they weren't using it for intentional ministry. Instead, it was an informal gathering place with low engagement and virtually no growth. I asked them how they let people know about it, and they admitted people found it on their own since the church didn't promote it or discuss it publicly. As we planned the transition of the group into their online church campus, I encouraged them to approach the change with the same level of excitement they would bring to launching a new physical location.

The leaders were a bit skeptical about having a launch event since the group already existed, so we decided the better approach would be to brand it as a relaunch. The campus leaders turned off group posts for a couple of weeks before the relaunch and advertised in the group and on the page that something new was coming. They decided to hold their relaunch during their midweek worship service, and I remember them saying they didn't expect to get any new group members that night.

The pastors, leaders, worship leaders, greeters, and everyone serving that night wore blue Facebook shirts to raise awareness about the campus relaunch. The pastor so effectively conveyed his vision for the campus that despite anticipating no new members that night, *235 people joined*. Not only that, but the campus activity level shot through the roof as people posted pictures from the event and introduced themselves in the group. As more people joined, they invited friends and family to join, doubling the campus size in one week.

Takeaway

Campuses that grow steadily make sure people know it's more than just an extension of *your* church; it's *their own tool* for evangelism. As you launch your Facebook campus, invite people into the vision. Make it clear that you need their help to extend the reach of the church. You should also get into the practice of making the invitation to join your Facebook campus part of your regular invitation to

Campuses that grow steadily make sure people know It's more than just an extension of *your* church; it's *their own tool* for evangelism.

join your church (in real life). This will help people make the shift from thinking, "Church happens at a building" to "Church happens in community." A strong Facebook campus launch will set you up for long-term impact if you follow a strong launch with strong leadership. And that's our next discussion.

CHAPTER 9

Leading Your
Facebook Campus

S he had spent every waking moment of their ten-month engagement obsessing about this day. And it had finally arrived. Every detail of her wedding day had been lovingly and meticulously planned, and so far, all was going as scheduled. Her father helped her out of a white 1950 Rolls-Royce to begin her walk toward the church doors. A crowd of family and friends awaited her inside. She nervously glanced back at the car window to catch a final glimpse of herself to make sure everything was perfect.

When the wedding coordinator saw the bride making her way toward the doors, she signaled in her walkie-talkie for the orchestra to begin playing part of Richard Wagner's 1850 opera, the "Bridal Chorus" in B-flat major, better known as "Here Comes the Bride." Everyone stood and looked toward the doors in anticipation. When the doors opened, everyone inhaled deeply and sucked the oxygen out of the room. There she was. A vision of perfection. The lights dimmed as a spotlight shone directly onto her and her father, following their every step down the aisle as she made her way to the altar. At last she turned to her father, and he turned to her as the preacher asked, "Who gives this woman to be married today?" And her father, with a tear in his eye, said, "I do." But as he placed her hand into the hand of the groom, she suddenly pulled it back and yelled, "Wait! I don't want to get married *for real*! I just wanted my dream wedding!" And with that, she turned and ran out of the church.

This scene is fictional, but given that so many marriages end in divorce, the data would say it isn't far-fetched. When it comes to new ventures, how often do we want the wedding but not the marriage? In other words, how often do we want the fun without the work? It's easy to plan for a campus launch day, but the purpose of the launch is *to lead* the people. I've witnessed many churches get excited about launching a Facebook campus. Still, they've done it without the appropriate staffing or resources to sustain it much beyond that day (even when I've advised them of what it takes to be successful). Many marriages have failed

It's easy to plan for a campus launch day, but the purpose of the launch is *to lead* the people.

because more energy was invested in the wedding than in the marriage. This chapter is provided for Facebook campus pastors to help you lead your Facebook campus after the launch. Because that is when ministry will really happen.

Leading Your Leaders

I want to begin with the idea of leading your leaders. More important than growing the group or engaging people in the group is fostering the right culture within the team helping you lead the group. I want you first to commit yourself to resisting the temptation to lower your standards for people you appoint to help you shepherd the Facebook campus. If you bring someone onto your team only because they're on Facebook a lot and have free time, those aren't good enough reasons. You should use as much discretion for your Facebook campus leadership team as you would for real-life hires. Remember, your Facebook campus is filled with real people. Your team, whether paid or volunteer, needs to be people whom you would hire to work alongside you if you were launching and leading a new physical location.

Although your team may encompass people in different cities, states, and time zones, I suggest you find a time once a week when you can all spend thirty minutes to an hour together to pray. Remind everyone of the vision and mission of the group, and discuss important updates, member stories, and ministry opportunities. It may be that Facebook released a new group tool and you want everyone to know how to use it, or it may be that the senior/lead pastor wants church staff to be united in a specific prayer for the church,

129

Regular touchpoints with the team are important for cohesion.

or it may be that a lot of questions are being asked in the group about the Holy Spirit and that presents an opportunity to do a new teaching unit about it. Whatever the case, regular touchpoints with the team are important for cohesion.

Campus Infrastructure

There isn't a hard-and-fast rule about how best to structure your team, but I suggest the following as a frame of reference for purposes of ministry:

Facebook Campus Pastor
Facebook Director of Men
Facebook Director of Women
Facebook Director of Youth
Facebook Director of Parents
Facebook Director of Singles
Facebook Director of Married Couples

Each director should be made a group administrator, and they should identify one or two people who can serve on their team as ministry managers at the group moderator level. The director's role is to know how many in the group are within their scope of ministry and to deepen relationships *with* them while facilitating relationships *among* them. The directors are also responsible for ensuring that the people in their scope of ministry are getting what they need from the group. This is the core leadership team I suggest you appoint at the beginning. It can grow as your group membership grows or be shaped differently to meet emerging needs.

Doing Discipleship

I shared at the beginning of this book that discipleship is the process of coming alongside people in an intentional way to enable them to grow and mature in their faith. As your group increases in size, the prospect of coming alongside people can feel a bit overwhelming. I've worked with churches whose groups grew to more than fifty thousand people, so I understand the feeling of unwieldiness that

Discipleship is the process of coming alongside people in an intentional way to enable them to grow and **mature in their faith.**

can come at that scale. But the truth is that whether your group is fifty thousand people or fifty, you want it to be a place where discipleship happens, so having a solid infrastructure in place that leverages the tools available to you will make it easier. Here are some of the tools in Facebook groups that can facilitate discipleship.

UNITS

One of the best tools for discipleship in groups (in my humble opinion) is the learning units feature, a feature available when you choose "social learning" as your group type. This is why I recommended that type when setting up the group. With learning units, you can create structured learning modules for group members to take, which is a great way to help people work through doctrine, tenets of the faith, and even real-life challenges. You can create learning units to supplement sermon series, and you can create learning units to orient people to your church culture and goals. The various ways you can use this tool is limited only by your imagination, so try it out and make it a central part of your group's discipleship strategy. Once you make the group a "social learning" group, you will be able to build modules on the units tab from your laptop or desktop. There are several great resources available through the Facebook help center and YouTube to aid you in learning how to do it. And a great bonus is that, with units, you can see how many people are progressing through the learning curriculum at any given time and can see who didn't complete the unit. This information is a great opportunity for personal encouragement and follow-up.

TOPIC TAGS

You will find that people ask the same questions pretty regularly in the group: "Where's everyone live?" "Any dads here?" "Any recommendations on a good place to eat in Baltimore?" This isn't ill-intentioned; it's simply the result of missing information. With topic tags, you can tag posts to better organize them under a common theme, especially when posts offer quality information on common interests. You don't have to tag all posts, and I don't recommend that you do. You currently can add a maximum of 150 topic categories, but the average for most groups is no more than thirty. Some suggested tags for your Facebook campus are prayer requests, fasting, forgiveness, serving, giving, depression, leadership, parenting, sex and love, and Q&A with a pastor. As with most advice in this book, you should use this feature in whatever way is best for your church. Be creative, but most important, be relevant.

FACEBOOK LIVE TEACHING

The Facebook Live feature is one of the best tools for providing opportunities for discipleship. It's also a great tool for humanizing the group. Posts are wonderful, and the ensuing comment threads can be insightful, but there's nothing like when a person pops up in the group, and you tune in and say, "Hey, Nona! Thanks for joining." Once a person has been seen and recognized, it's also a bit more difficult for them to leave. I've built a couple of Facebook Live suggestions into the weekly engagement calendar, with the first one being "Monday Night Live with Pastor [Name]."

This idea was born out of my own experience as a

preacher. Once I leave the pulpit, there's a lingering question in my mind: "Did they get it?" My husband and I would regularly have that conversation during our drive home from worship, and no matter what *we* think the answer is, there's only one way to know for sure: *ask them*. Monday Night Live is a chance to connect with everyone for thirty minutes to an hour and take their questions. Simply post after Sunday worship asking people for questions and reactions to the sermon, then work through that list live Monday evening. You should also take any live questions people post that night. It's a great way to come alongside people and make sure they really understand what God is saying through you.

Another great way to use Facebook Live is to do a teaching based on conversations you see happening in the group. Let's say someone posted something that can be classified as gossip. The first temptation would be to remove that post and chastise the person. Instead, do what Jesus always did. He recognized personal failures as teachable moments. He gathered together whoever would listen to share a truth that helped the entire listening population grow, not only the person who needed the lesson. It's a privilege to help the entire group grow in their faith, so use Facebook Live to help you do that.

ROOMS

We all know that church doesn't stop at the end of the weekend gathering. Church isn't a program; it's a community of people who are growing in faith together under the lordship of Jesus Christ. Rooms was introduced during COVID-19 as a response to the need for small groups of people to connect through video chat. It is a powerful way to keep small groups working together during the week and is an important ministry tool for churches desiring to create spaces within Facebook for members to connect and grow. As a relatively new feature, it will continue to be enhanced over time but is already showing promising results as a lever for deeper connection within churches.

GROUP ANALYTICS

I'm a data person. I love numbers. If your group reaches 250 members, you will unlock the group analytics tool, which will give you a rich data picture of how your group performs over time. This data should be used to help you deepen your impact, so review it regularly with your campus leadership team and your senior/lead pastor. Some of the insights you will receive include:

> **Top Contributors:** These are the people making posts and keeping the conversation going. Reward them by establishing a weekly post recognizing top contributors and sending them a thank-you gift such as a church T-shirt or a Starbucks gift card.
>
> **Top Posts:** This will tell you which posts are generating the most reactions and comments. Review these posts to better understand the topics and themes that mean the most to people.
>
> **Time of Day:** This statistic will let you know when your people are on Facebook. There is nothing like scheduling an important post for 3:00 p.m. only to receive no reactions or comments. Knowing when

people are there is important for optimizing the number of eyes on your posts.

Geography: As your group grows, geography data will let you know where people live so you can plan offline events that connect people in real life. For a church I work with in Texas, their second-largest geographic campus membership is Nigeria. Without this insight, they would have never known they needed an in-person ministry there.

Taking It Offline

As you learn more about the geographic distribution of your members, it will be important to remember that your Facebook campus is simply a vehicle for ministry. It isn't the destination. While you can do incredible and impactful work in the group, fostering real-life connections will be the pure gold of your online campus. You can set a day and time every month where you encourage group members to meet up offline for a get-together in their area. It can be as simple as prayer at the park, where you host a prayer gathering at a local park, followed by breakfast or lunch.

Fostering real-life connections will be the pure gold of your online campus.

Build a **leadership infrastructure** to make sure the events meet your church's standards.

You could also plan a Facebook campus service day, where you encourage people to organize local service projects that extend the reach and impact of the group into their local communities. You can also encourage people to get together just to have fun: go skating or fishing or bowling. The options are endless, and the goal is simply to drive in-person connections. While an online "I'm praying for you" is nice, there's nothing like sitting beside the person, holding their hand, and praying together.

A note of caution here. As you venture into hosting offline events through your campus, you should build a leadership infrastructure to make sure the events meet your church's standards. You may appoint volunteers as local event coordinators, but if you do, you should make sure they receive the same level of training you would provide to event coordinators at a physical location.

Keeping Your Campus Safe

One of the principle responsibilities of the Facebook campus pastor will be to keep the Facebook campus culture healthy, and that will happen only if you can also keep it safe. I want to make you aware of a few key safety controls you can use to promote safety in your group.

- Use the "private" privacy setting to ensure that only members can see group posts.
- Explicitly tell people that they will be removed if they screenshot a group post and make it public. Actually remove them if they do, and let everyone know that you did.
- If you'd like more control over your membership, turn on membership approval, and make it clear that all new members will require approval by an admin or moderator.
- If a conversation is headed in the wrong direction, turn off post commenting to help the situation cool down.
- Tell members they can report objectionable posts and comments to campus leadership.
- Create a post that encourages members to help you keep the group safe.

And now, with these ideas tucked away in your heart, I want to pivot to our last focal area: growing your group.

CHAPTER 10

Growing Your Campus

If you plant a seed in good soil, water it, and provide nutrients, it will grow into whatever plant, fruit, or vegetable it was intended to be. You don't need gimmicks, strategies, or innovations to make the seed grow; you only need to provide the necessary requirements to support life, and it will grow on its own. I look at my two young sons and see this truth played out in living color every day. My oldest is nine; he was born at twenty-six weeks of pregnancy, weighed 2 pounds, 9 ounces, and was 13 inches long. He spent the first three months of his life in a neonatal intensive care unit (NICU), fighting to live. Every day brought a new medical challenge, and my husband and I couldn't do anything to help him. But we did the most important thing: we prayed and let the doctors do their jobs. Our boy had many ups and downs during his ninety days in the NICU, but what gave his medical team the most comfort was his growth. As he gained weight and grew taller over time, they saw that as a sign that his body was responding appropriately to the interventions and nutrition they provided him.

Every pastor and church leader I've consulted with has raised the question of growth when planning for a Facebook campus launch. The underlying assumption is that growing a real-life church and growing a digital church must require different approaches since their nature is different. I've discovered, however, that a physical church and a digital church are governed by the exact same principles when it comes to growth, because a digital church is filled with real people. As you prepare to launch and lead your Facebook campus, you should first consider what has helped your physical church attendance or membership grow (or not). Do you use an email distribution list to raise awareness? Do you go door to door? Do you send postcards? Do you host special events? To the best of your ability, extend those good practices to your online church, and refrain from implementing practices that have stifled growth offline.

The following best practices for growing your Facebook campus can be leveraged to grow your physical attendance because growth isn't a destination; it's a journey. And the journey is fueled by one thing: engagement.

A digital church is filled with real people.

Engage People

After working with countless churches to launch Facebook campuses, I have noticed that the ones that have failed have done so because of an absence of engagement. The group was treated as just another content distribution channel instead of a living, breathing community of people. I sincerely hope your ushers or greeters don't throw event flyers at attendees as they walk into your building each weekend. Still, I can't tell you how many times I've seen event posts be the only content tossed at people in a group. To take a different approach, here are a few things you can do to make your Facebook campus an engaging place to be.

- **Welcome people when they join.** This is such a simple gesture that most churches have built a process around welcoming new people who join their physical church. Now we simply need to extend it to Facebook. Ask new group members a question, or invite them to introduce themselves. By engaging with them directly, you let them know you see and value them and that they chose to join the right church community.
- **Help members understand what the group is for.** A short post that gives some examples of what people can share and discuss helps new members get acclimated. Better yet, create a unit for new members that takes them through basic information about your church, such as your vision, what it means to be a Christian, and how they can participate in the

141

Facebook campus. This will be the digital corollary to your real-life new-member assimilation process.

- **Encourage members to invite friends.** Just as you would for a physical location, grow your Facebook campus through your existing members. Encourage them to add friends with a post that reminds them what the group is for and clarifies who the ideal member would be. You can even incentivize this with a contest that has prizes for people who invite the most members.

- **Ask questions.** Questions are a fun, direct way to invite conversation. Simply ask people to share their thoughts on a given topic. Even asking them to share something as informal as what they're up to can be a great way to get the group talking. To make the group feel especially supportive, be vulnerable when posing a question and share your own struggles before asking others to do the same.

- **Tag people in posts.** If you want to hear from someone, tag them in your post using the @ symbol. It's a direct way to heighten post visibility for specific people so that they'll check in—and it will let them know you're thinking of them.

- **Comment on posts by members.** Let people know you're paying attention to them and what they share. Commenting on posts, even just to acknowledge you're happy they posted, encourages members to post again.

- **Collaborate with polls, docs, events, and Facebook Live.** Get input from your members with a poll, work together in a shared document, and help organize activities with Facebook events, or have discussions in real time with Facebook Live.

Promote the Group

One of the most basic requirements for your Facebook campus to grow is for people to be made aware of its existence. Here are a few suggestions that have worked well for the churches I have consulted with.

Link to Your Page: Although this is listed as a step in the Facebook campus launch plan, I want to reemphasize it here just in case you missed it. When you create the group, you should link it to your church page by going into page settings and selecting "Link Group" so that people will be able to discover it through your page. You can link up to 250 groups to your page, and once they're linked, you can choose to add a call-to-action button to your page that says "Visit Group." You can designate which group people land on upon clicking the button. They will still have to request to join the group in order to view the content and participate in conversations, but the button will direct them to where you want them to go first.

Advertise the Group: Facebook ads are one of the most effective, low-cost means by which you can spread the word about your group. By targeting specific ages, geographic locations, and other demographic variables, you can reach your intended audience without breaking the bank. A ten-dollar ad can reach thousands of people, so leverage this tool in partnership with your marketing and communications teams. In the absence of that resource, you can take the *free* Facebook Blueprint course (available online) to learn everything you need to know about marketing and advertising on Facebook. Simply share the group to your page and advertise the post it creates.

Platform Promotion: Every week, you have the opportunity to invite people to join your Facebook campus. Use it. As people join and find it to be a meaningful part of their lives, they will invite friends and family to join as well. I've seen countless examples of people joining a church's Facebook campus and then eventually showing up at a building to connect with the church offline. If you use time in the pulpit each week to ask people to invite friends to church, make sure you include the invitation to join your church without walls.

Member Invitations: Encourage people to invite their friends and family to join the group. You might even offer inexpensive prizes for people who get the most friends to join over a week. This may be an administrative challenge initially because you will have to manually keep track of who invited people, but it will eventually reap dividends as more people discover and connect with your church.

Website and Email: Create space on your website to invite people to join your Facebook campus by clicking a button that opens in a new window with the URL of your group. Similarly, include a button in your enewsletter that invites people to join the group, and update your email signatures to include a link to join your Facebook group.

Marketing Collateral: Marketing materials can help promote your group. Below are a few ideas:

- *Printed bulletins*: Include the web address to join your Facebook campus, or create a QR code that people can scan.

- *Posters*: Raise awareness about your Facebook campus through posters strategically placed throughout your property.

- *Text blasts*: Send a text blast to all members with a link to join your Facebook campus.

- *Sign-up stations*: Set your Facebook campus as the home page at church computer stations in high-traffic areas.

Making It Real

The church was small by most standards. They saw about one hundred people during their service every Sunday morning—150 if it was a special Sunday. When I met with the pastor about launching a Facebook campus, he was amused by the idea but didn't think it was necessary. "We know each other. We have each other's phone numbers and know where we all live. We don't need a Facebook group." My question to him was simple: "Do you believe you've reached the maximum capacity of God's vision for your ministry?" He looked stumped. He paused, turned to look out the window for a moment, and then said, "Honestly? I haven't thought much about vision. I think I've gotten comfortable with what's familiar." After fifteen more minutes of conversation, he relented and said he would be willing to give a Facebook group a try, but he didn't expect much.

Although I wanted to do a Facebook campus launch event, the pastor didn't want to do anything too big for fear of making a big deal about something that wouldn't work. Instead, I convinced him to spend one hundred dollars over three weeks on Facebook ads promoting his new campus. He chose not to say anything about the group from the pulpit and instead had an announcement placed in the bulletin. The Sunday after the bulletin announcement, twenty-three people joined the group, and by that Wednesday, the group was up to seventy-two. He ran his first Facebook ad about the church's new Facebook campus the next Friday. By the next Sunday, the group was at 146 people.

As he looked out into the sanctuary of eighty-two,

he realized that the power of what was happening on Facebook was beyond what he thought possible. When he called me the next day, I could hear something in his voice that excited me. It was hope. It was energy. It was vision. "Nona, I have to be honest. I didn't give much thought to this Facebook campus thing, but I see something taking place that's really special. How do I take this to the next level? What do I do? You've really inspired me."

I had worked with many of the largest churches in America and around the world, but that pastor, the one who had been discouraged for so long that he no longer had a vision for his church, inspired me to write the book you now hold in your hands. Sometimes discovering the possibility for growing your church is all the inspiration we need to once again believe in what God can do.

For the Kingdom: Final Thoughts

Everyone wants to be successful in what they do, but I've come to believe that many of us define success wrong. I'm no exception. For many years of my career, I defined my success on the basis of my title, where I sat on an org chart, and what my salary was. I defined it by which exclusive parties I got invited to and which big-ticket platforms I was asked to speak on. By the time I turned thirty-five, I had achieved more in my career than most dream of achieving in a lifetime, but it still wasn't enough. I would find myself comparing my station in life with those of people five or ten years older and end up feeling as if I still hadn't made it. The saddest part of it all is that I *know better*.

After being in ministry for almost twenty years, I know what the Bible says about riches, priorities, comparison, and foolishness. Yet knowing what the Bible says and living what the Bible says are two very different practices. One requires memorization, and the other requires internalization. When it comes to memory, mine is annoyingly sharp. I remember things I desperately want to forget. Yet as easily

Knowing what the Bible says and **living** what the Bible says are two very different practices.

as I can quote Scripture, I find myself struggling to live it. I know this is part of the human condition, but I'm saying this explicitly because I want to be super clear about my next point.

We are naturally drawn into the psychological game of comparing ourselves with others to determine our worth by proxy, and as pastors, we're not exempt. We all have other pastors, speakers, and churches we compare ourselves with to help us gauge whether we are successful. But a word of caution: no matter how large your physical church or Facebook campus grows, none of that matters if people aren't discovering and following Jesus *more than they're following you.* Hear me on this. One of the biggest dangers I've observed in working with some churches is that pastors and church leaders can fixate on increasing followers, engagement, and attenders without a corresponding fixation on growing disciples. I've even had a well-known pastor tell me, "Let's get to that discipleship stuff later. For now, just tell me how to increase my likes." No. No. No.

I said it in the introduction, and it bears repeating: it doesn't matter how many followers you have if the people following *you* don't ultimately follow *Jesus.* So my final thought to you is never to forget this is for the kingdom. And let me be extra clear—this is for *God's kingdom*. Don't fall into the trap of allowing people to make you feel like a king or queen whose domain is your church and whose loyal subjects are your members or attenders. Remember, social *media* is about marketing. Social *ministry* is about disciples. We have been called to make disciples, and social media is an unparalleled tool to allow us to do that at scale in this day and time. Use it for God's glory, and always reflect back to him the good it produces.

I am praying for you, cheering for you, and excited for you. Now make the leap!

It doesn't matter how many followers you have if the people following *you* don't ultimately **follow *Jesus*.**

Notes

1. "Becoming Five Multiplication Study: Research Report," LifeWay Research, February 2019, http://lifewayresearch.com /wp-content/uploads/2019/03/2019ExponentialReport.pdf.
2. The General Social Survey, http://gss.norc.org/getthedata
3. "The Most Post-Christian Cities in America: 2019," Barna Research Group, June 5, 2019, https://www.barna.com /research/post-christian-cities-2019/.
4. "In U.S., Decline of Christianity Continues at Rapid Pace," *Pew Research Center*, October 17, 2019, https:// www.pewforum.org/2019/10/17/in-u-s-decline -of-christianity-continues-at-rapid-pace/.
5. "Becoming Five Multiplication Study: Research Report," LifeWay Research, February 2019, http://lifewayresearch.com /wp-content/uploads/2019/03/2019ExponentialReport.pdf.
6. Frank Newport, "2017 Update on Americans and Religion," *Gallup*, December 22, 2017, http://news.gallup .com/poll/224642/2017-update-americans-religion.aspx.
7. Melissa G. Hunt et al., "No More FOMO: Limiting Social Media Decreases Loneliness and Depression," *Journal of Social and Clinical Psychology* vol. 37, no. 10 (2018): 751–68, https://guilfordjournals.com/doi/pdf/10.1521/jscp .2018.37.10.751.
8. Kristin Long, "Infographic: Why Visual Content Is Better

Than Text," *Ragan*, April 11, 2014, https://www.ragan.com/infographic-why-visual-content-is-better-than-text/.

9. "Distribution of Facebook Users Worldwide as of October 2019, By Age and Gender," Statista, October 2019, https://www.statista.com/statistics/376128/facebook-global-user-age-distribution/.

10. Melissa G. Hunt et al., "No More FOMO: Limiting Social Media Decreases Loneliness and Depression," *Journal of Social and Clinical Psychology* vol. 37, no. 10 (2018): 751–68, https://guilfordjournals.com/doi/pdf/10.1521/jscp.2018.37.10.751.

11. Stephen Covey, *The Seven Habits of Highly Effective People: Powerful Lessons in Personal Change* (New York: Free Press, 2004), 95.

About the Author

Nona Jones is a rare combination of preacher, teacher, author, business executive, entrepreneur, media personality, and worship leader. She is internationally recognized as a leading expert in leveraging social media for discipleship and led the creation and implementation of the global faith-based partnerships strategy for the world's largest social network. She's served as a thought partner to church and denominational leaders around the world to make digital discipleship part of their holistic ministry model.

Prior to Facebook, Nona held executive roles across the public, private, and nonprofit sectors. She received the American Public Power Association's Robert F. Roundtree Rising Star Award as national peer recognition of her leadership while under the age of thirty-five and has been recognized by *Essence* magazine as one of their "Under 40 Women to Watch." She serves on the University of Florida Digital Advisory Council and is a graduate of Leadership Florida and the Presidential Leadership Scholars Program, a unique leadership development initiative led by President Bill Clinton and President George W. Bush.

In addition to Nona's professional and civic work, she leads a church in Gainesville, Florida, with her husband, Pastor Timothy Jones. She considers being the wife of Tim and mommy of Timothy Jr. and Isaac her greatest accomplishments in life.